PIANO · VOCAL · GUITAR

THE BIG BOOK OF
IRISH SONGS

ISBN 0-634-05847-9

HAL·LEONARD®
CORPORATION
7777 W. BLUEMOUND RD. P.O. BOX 13819 MILWAUKEE, WI 53213

Visit Hal Leonard Online at
www.halleonard.com

CONTENTS

THE BAND PLAYED ON

Words by JOHN E. PALMER
Music by CHARLES B. WARD

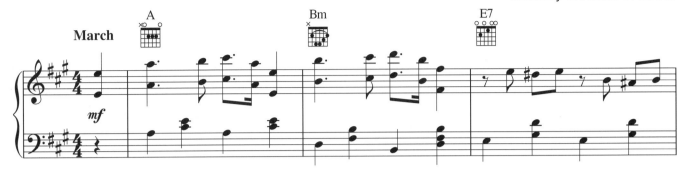

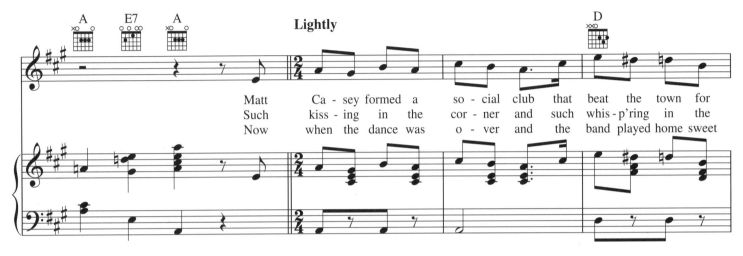

Matt Ca-sey formed a so-cial club that beat the town for
Such kiss-ing in the cor-ner and such whis-p'ring in the
Now when the dance was o-ver and the band played home sweet

style. And hired____ for a meet-ing place a hall.____
hall, and tell-ing tales of love be-hind the stairs.____
home, they played a tune at Ca-sey's own re-quest.____

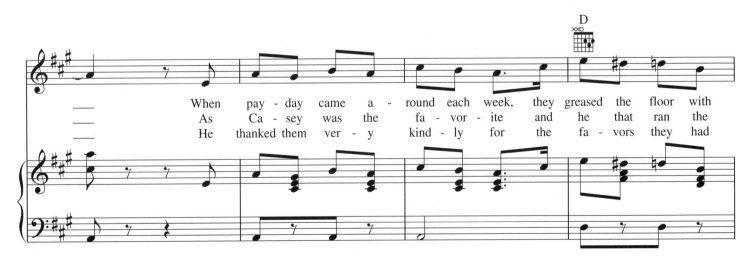

____ When pay-day came a-round each week, they greased the floor with
____ As Ca-sey was the fa-vor-ite and he that ran the
____ He thanked them ver-y kind-ly for the fa-vors they had

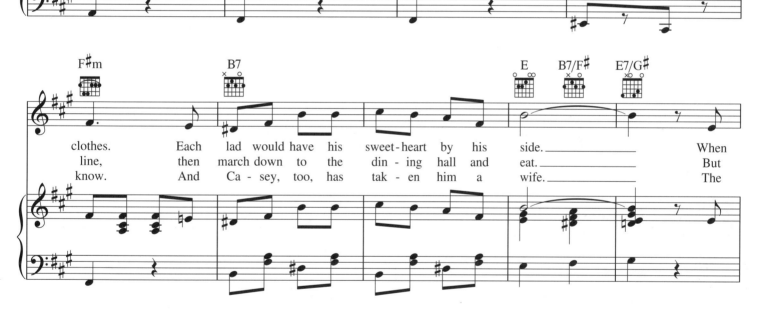

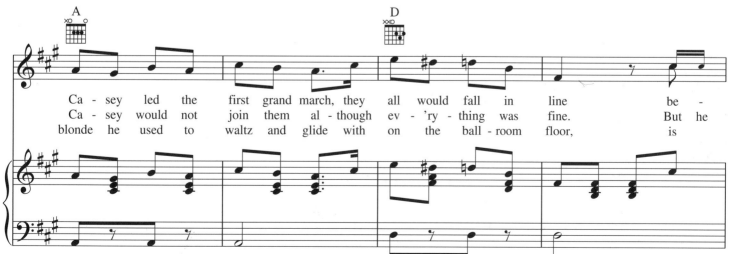

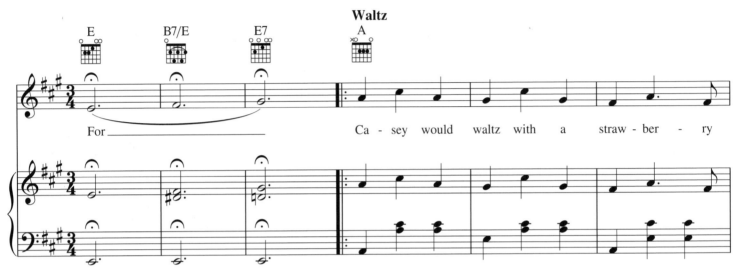

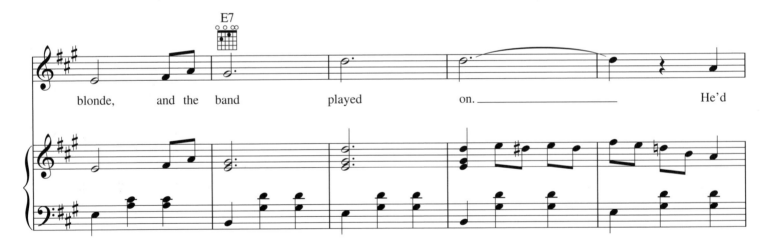

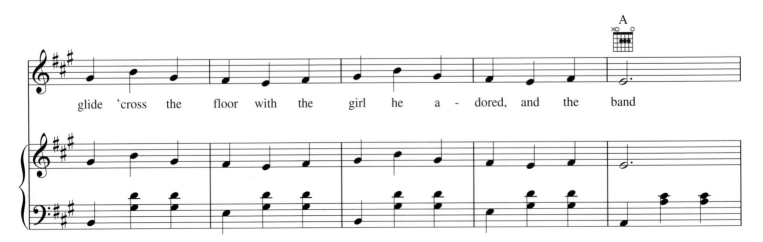

played on._____ But his brain was so load-ed it

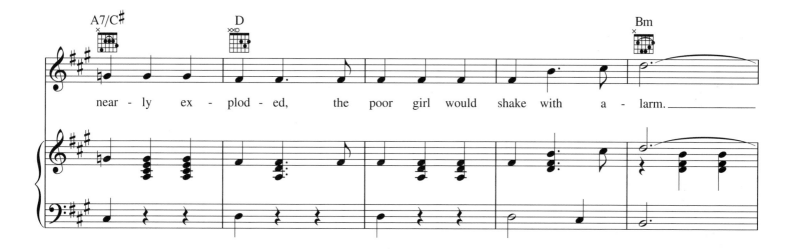

near-ly ex-plod-ed, the poor girl would shake with a-larm._____

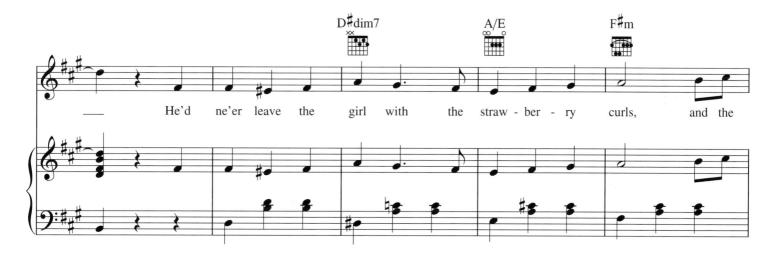

He'd ne'er leave the girl with the straw-ber-ry curls, and the

band played on._____ on._____

BELIEVE ME, IF ALL THOSE ENDEARING YOUNG CHARMS

Words and Music by
THOMAS MOORE

BENDEMEER'S STREAM

Traditional Irish Folk Melody
Words by THOMAS MOORE

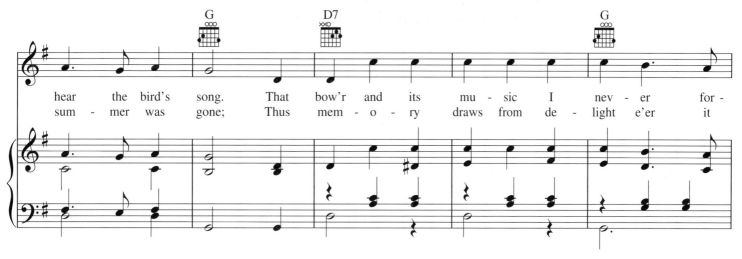

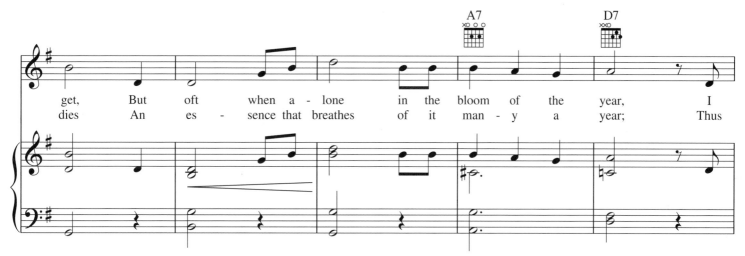

hear the bird's song. That bow'r and its mu - sic I nev - er for - get,
sum - mer was gone; Thus mem - o - ry draws from de - light e'er it dies

But oft when a - lone in the bloom of the year, I think, "Is the
An es - sence that breathes of it man - y a year; Thus bright to my

night - in - gale sing - ing there yet? Are the ros - es still bright by the calm Ben - de - meer?" No the
soul as 'twas then to my eyes, Is that bow'r on the banks of the calm Ben - de - meer!

BLACK VELVET BAND

Traditional Irish Folksong

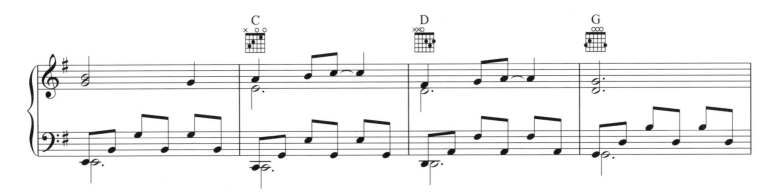

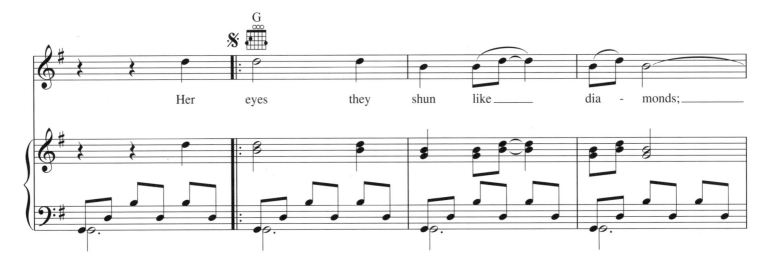

Her eyes they shun like ____ dia - monds; ____

____ you'd think she was queen of the land. ____

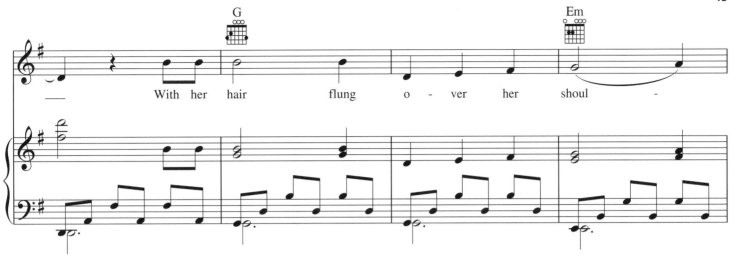

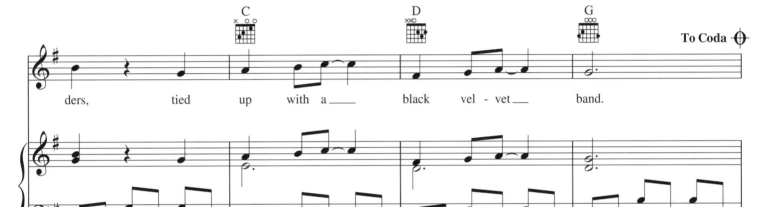

With her hair flung o - ver her shoul - ders, tied up with a ___ black vel - vet ___ band.

To Coda

As I ___ went walk - ing down ___ Broad - way, ___
'Fore judge ___ and ju - ry next ___ morn - ing ___

not in - tend - ing to stay ver - y ___ long, ___
both of us did ___ ap - pear. ___

I met with this__ frol - ick - some dam -
A gen - tle - man__ claimed his_____ jew - el -

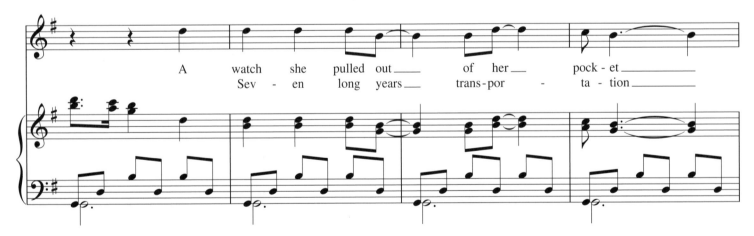

sel ry as she____ came trip - ping a - long._____
ry and the case a - gainst us was clear._____

A watch she pulled out__ of her__ pock - et_____
Sev - en long years__ trans - por - ta - tion_____

and slipped it right_ in - to me__ hand._____
right on down to__ Van Die - men's_ Land;_____

On the ver - y first day that I ___ met ___
far a - way from my friends and com - pan ___

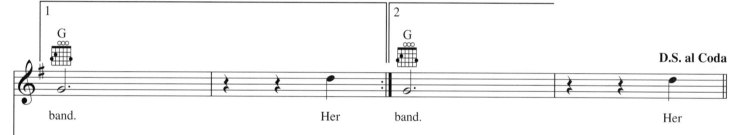

her, bad luck to her ___ black vel - vet ___
ions to fol - low the ___ black vel - vet ___

D.S. al Coda

band. Her band. Her

CODA

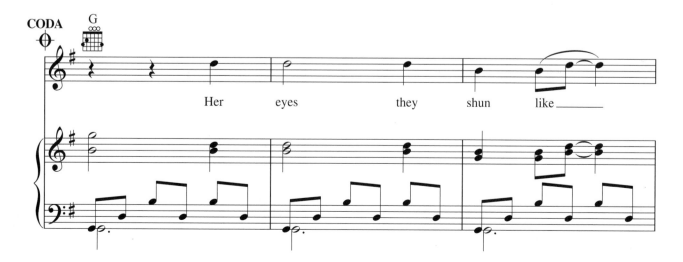

Her eyes they shun like ___

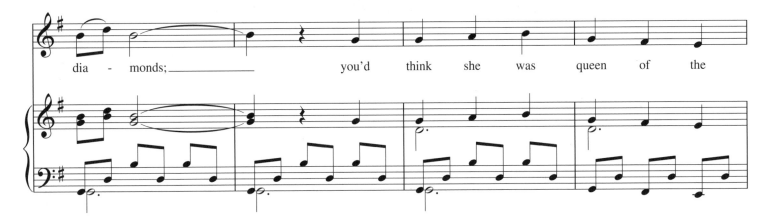

dia - monds; _____ you'd think she was queen of the

land. _____ With her hair flung

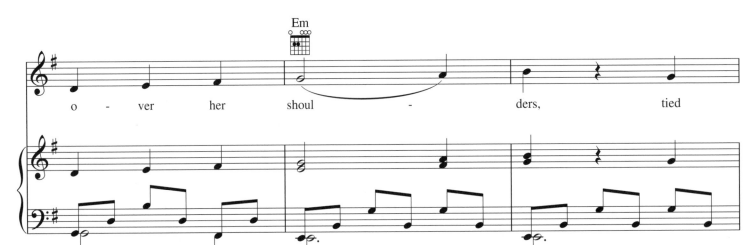

o - ver her shoul - ders, tied

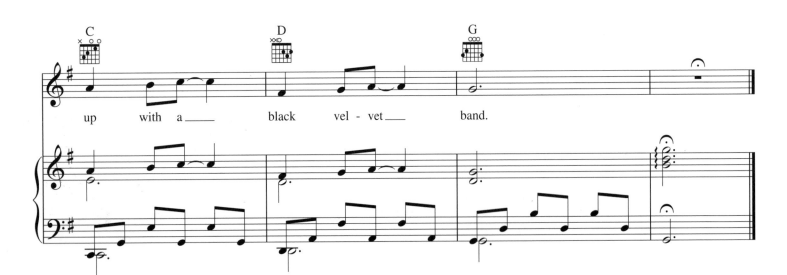

up with a ___ black vel - vet ___ band.

BOLD FENIAN MEN

Traditional Irish Folk Melody
Words by M. SCANLAN

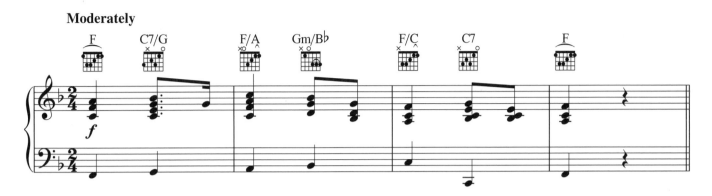

See who comes o - ver the red blos - somed heath - er, their
prayers and our tears they have scoffed and de - rid - ed. They've
men from the Nore, from the Suir and the Shan - non. Let

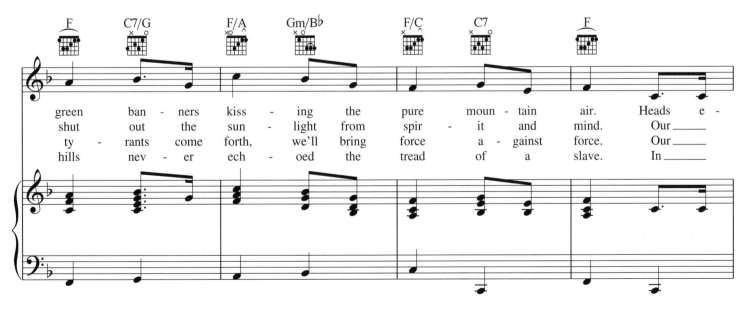

green ban - ners kiss - ing the pure moun - tain air. Heads e -
shut out the sun - light from spir - it and mind. Our _____
ty - rants come forth, we'll bring force a - gainst force. Our _____
hills nev - er ech - oed the tread of a slave. In _____

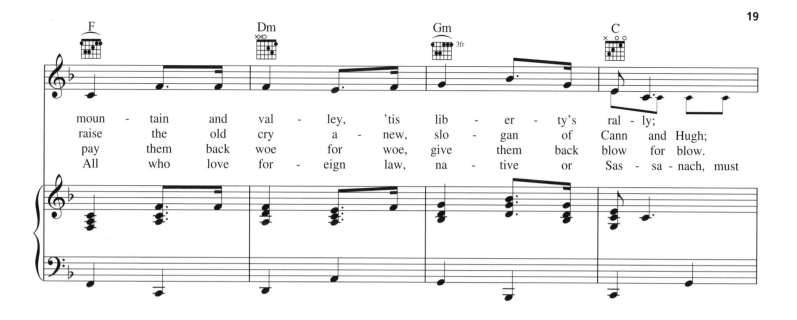

moun - tain and val - ley, 'tis lib - er - ty's ral - ly;
raise the old cry a - new, slo - gan of Cann and Hugh;
pay them old back woe for woe, give them back blow for blow.
All who love for - eign law, na - tive or Sas - sa - nach, must

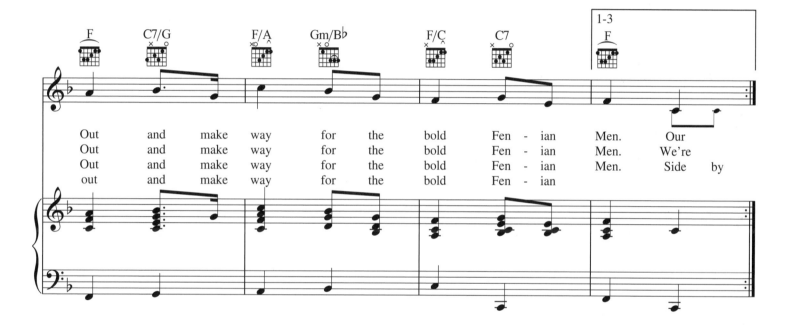

Out and make way for the bold Fen - ian Men. Our
Out and make way for the bold Fen - ian Men. We're
Out and make way for the bold Fen - ian Men. Side by
out and make way for the bold Fen - ian

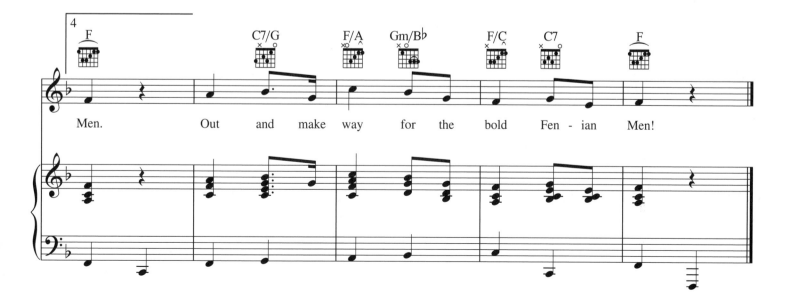

Men. Out and make way for the bold Fen - ian Men!

THE BOLD TENANT FARMER

Traditional Irish Folksong

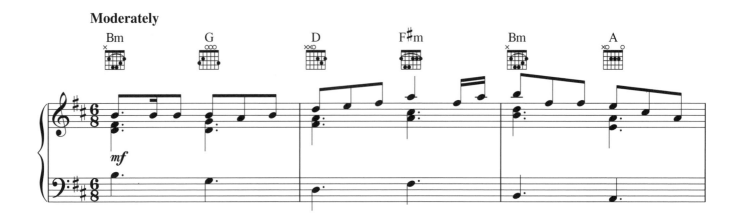

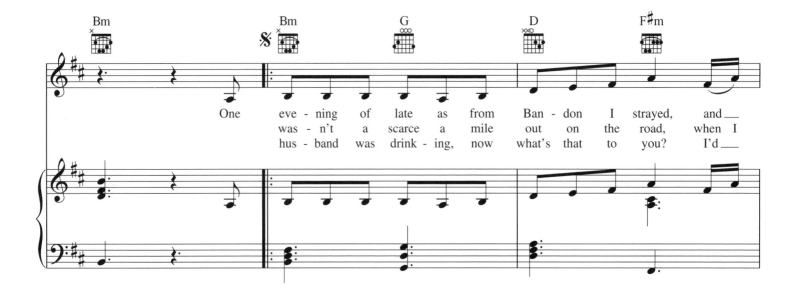

One eve - ning of late as from Ban - don I strayed, and ___
was - n't a scarce a mile out on the road, when I
hus - band was drink - ing, now what's that to you? I'd ___

towards Bal - lin - ga - ry I made a near way, and in Bal - lin - spid - dal I
heard a great fight in a farm - er's a - bode, by the son of a land - lord, an
rath - er he drink it than give it to you. You hun - gry old mi - ser, you're

made a de - lay, when I wet - ted my whis - tle with por - ter. I
ill - look - ing toad, and the wife of a poor ten - ant farm - er. "Oh,
not worth a chew, and your moss - y old land is no bar - gain." He

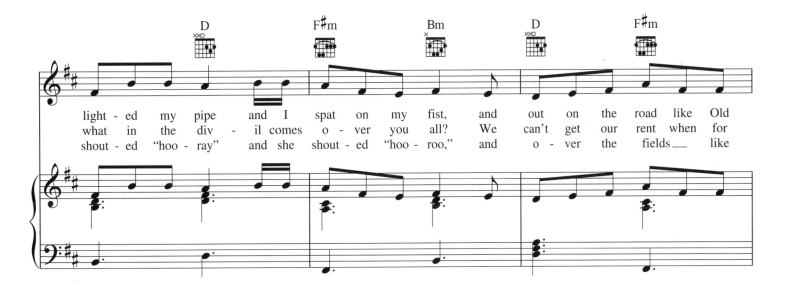

light - ed my pipe and I spat on my fist, and out on the road like Old
what in the div - il comes o - ver you all? We can't get our rent when for
shout - ed "hoo - ray" and she shout - ed "hoo - roo," and o - ver the fields___ like

Nick I did twist. Say - ing, "I care for no land - lord, no bail - iff or miss, but I'm
it we do call, but sure at next ses - sions you'll pay for it all, or you'll
Old Nick he flew. Say - ing, "May God help the land - lords and old Ire - land too!" A - gus

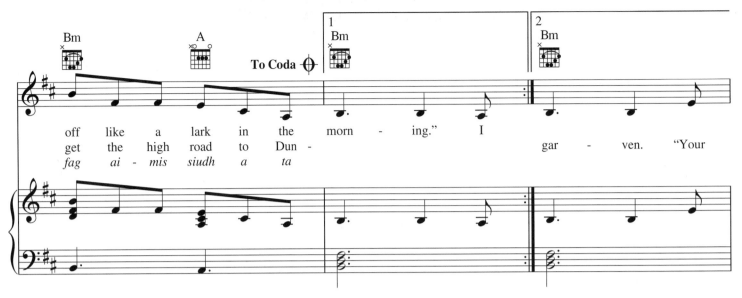

off like a lark in the morn - ing." I
get the high road to Dun - gar - ven. "Your
fag ai - mis siudh a ta

hus - band was drink - ing in town t'oth - er night, and shout - ing and fight - ing for

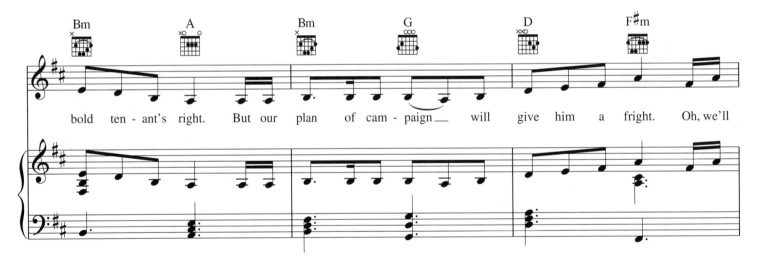

bold ten - ant's right. But our plan of cam - paign___ will give him a fright. Oh, we'll

bear ev - 'ry wind in your storm." "If my

se!

BOULAVOGUE

Traditional Irish Folksong

Moderately, in one

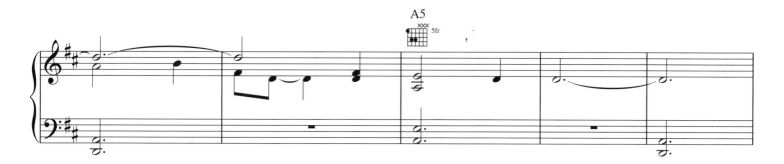

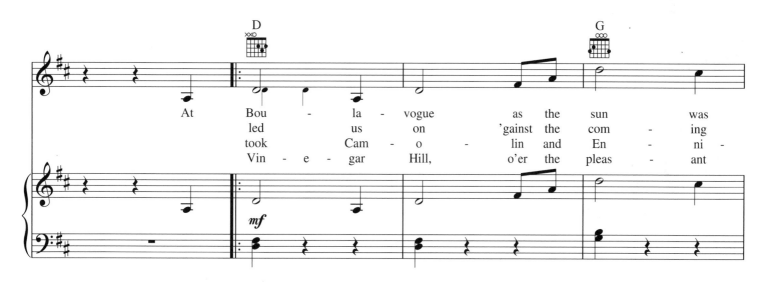

At Bou - la - vogue as the sun was
led us on 'gainst the com - ing
took Cam - o - lin and En - ni -
Vin - e - gar Hill, o'er the pleas - ant

set - ing ___ O'er bright May mead - ows ___ of Shel - ma -
sol - diers, ___ And the cow'rd - ly Yeo - men ___ were put to
scor - thy ___ And Wex - ford storm - ing, ___ drove out our
Sla - ney, ___ Our he - roes vain - ly ___ stood back to

CARRICKFERGUS

Traditional Irish Folksong

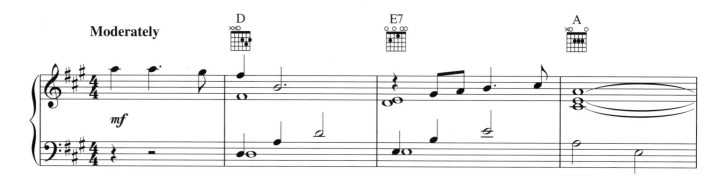

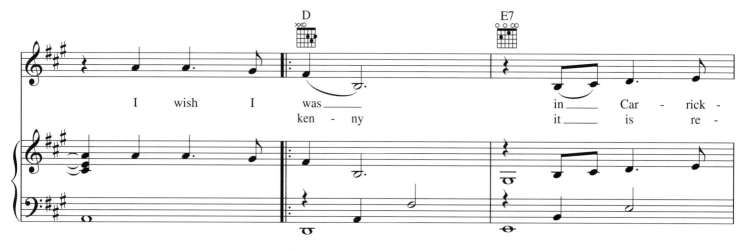

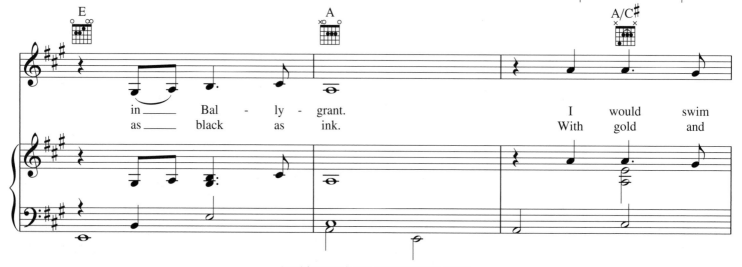

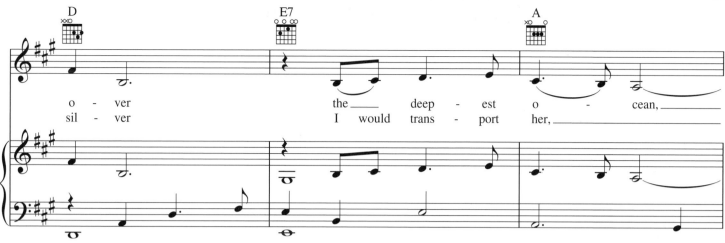

o - ver the____ deep - est o - cean,____
sil - ver I would trans - port her,____

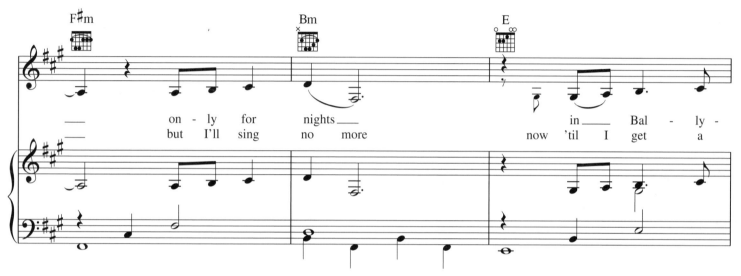

____ on - ly for nights____ in____ Bal - ly a
____ but I'll sing no more now 'til I get a

grant. But the sea is wide____ nor have____
drink. I'm____ drunk to - day,____ a hand - some

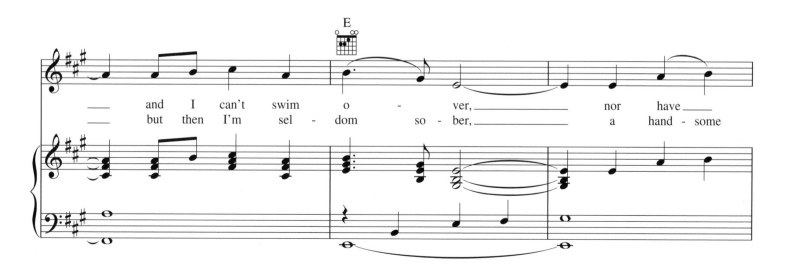

and I can't swim o - ver,____
but then I'm sel - dom so - ber,____

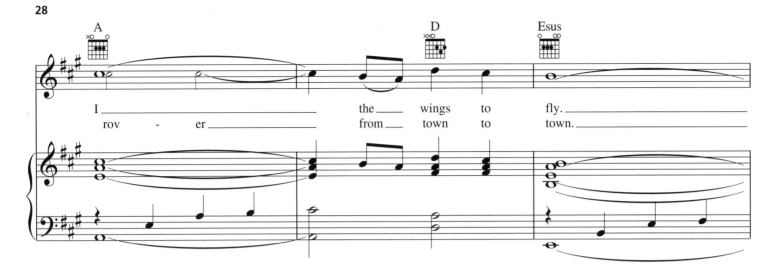

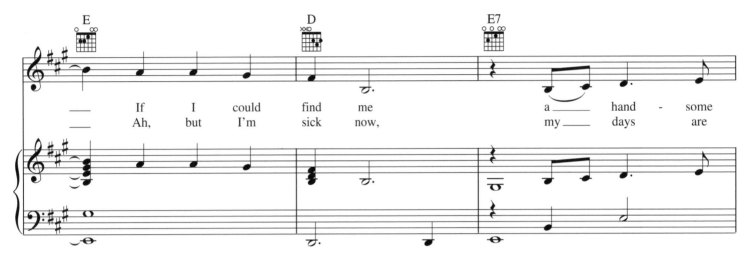

COME BACK TO ERIN

Traditional Irish Folksong

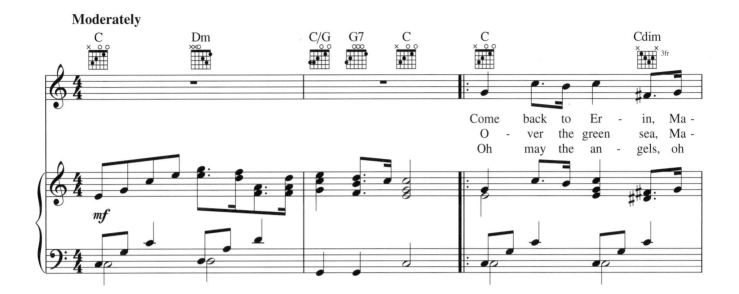

Come back to Er - in, Ma -
O - ver the green sea, Ma -
Oh may the an - gels, oh

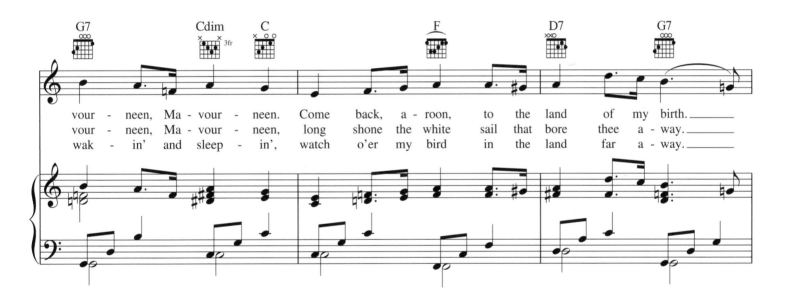

vour - neen, Ma - vour - neen. Come back, a - roon, to the land of my birth.
vour - neen, Ma - vour - neen, long shone the white sail that bore thee a - way.
wak - in' and sleep - in', watch o'er my bird in the land far a - way.

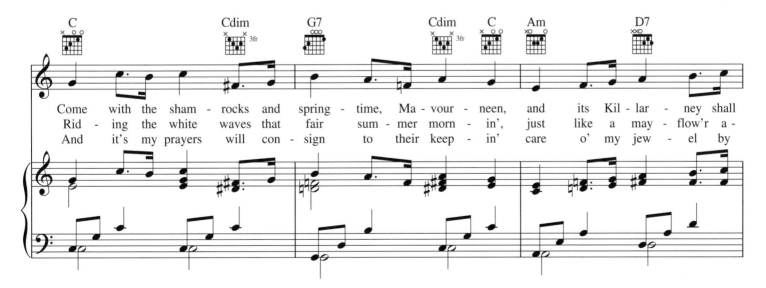

Come with the sham - rocks and spring - time, Ma - vour - neen, and its Kil - lar - ney shall
Rid - ing the white waves that fair sum - mer morn - in', just like a may - flow'r a -
And it's my prayers will con - sign to their keep - in' care o' my jew - el by

ring with our mirth. Sure, when we lent ye to beau - ti - ful Eng - land,
float on the bay. Oh, but my heart sank when clouds came be - tween us
night and by day. When by the fire - side I watch the bright em - bers,

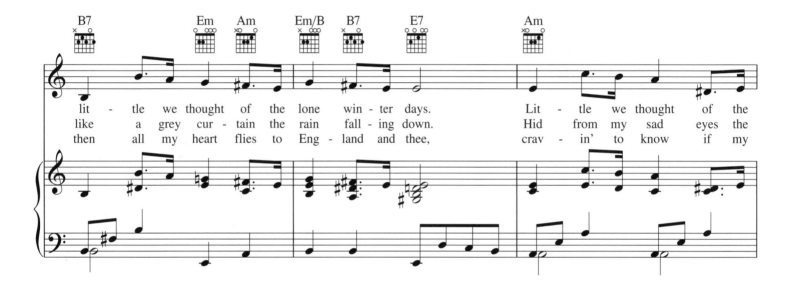

lit - tle we thought of the lone win - ter days. Lit - tle we thought of the
like a grey cur - tain the rain fall - ing down. Hid from my sad eyes the
then all my heart flies to Eng - land and thee, crav - in' to know if my

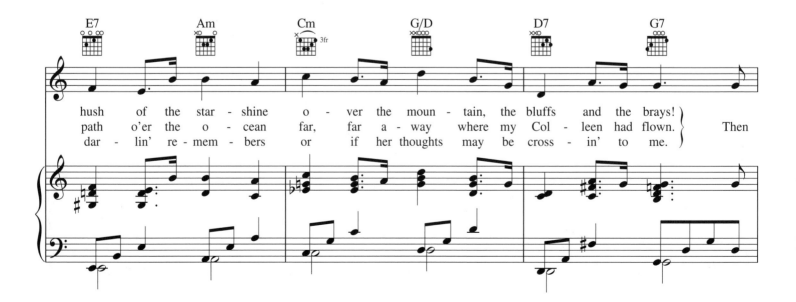

hush of the star - shine o - ver the moun - tain, the bluffs and the brays!
path o'er the o - cean far, far a - way where my Col - leen had flown. Then
dar - lin' re - mem - bers or if her thoughts may be cross - in' to me.

come back to Er - in, Ma - vour - neen, Ma - vour - neen. Come back a - gain to the

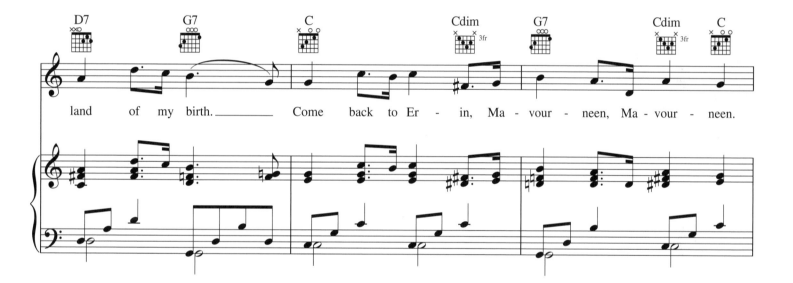

land of my birth.____ Come back to Er - in, Ma - vour - neen, Ma - vour - neen.

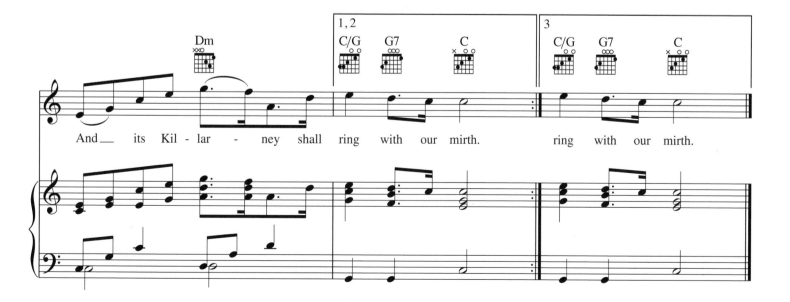

And__ its Kil - lar - ney shall ring with our mirth. ring with our mirth.

THE CRUISKEEN LAWN
(Cruiscín Lán)

Traditional Irish Folksong

DANNY BOY
(Londonderry Air)

Traditional Irish Folk Melody
Words by FREDERICK EDWARD WEATHERLY

back when sum-mer's in the mead - ow,____ or when the val - ley's hush'd and white with
hear, tho' soft your tread a - bove_ me,____ and all my dreams will warm and sweet - er

snow._____ 'Tis I'll be there in sun-shine or in shad - ow,_____ oh, Dan - ny
be._____ If you will not fail to tell me that you love_ me,_____ then I shall

Boy, oh Dan - ny Boy, I love you so! _____
sleep in peace un - til you come to me! _____

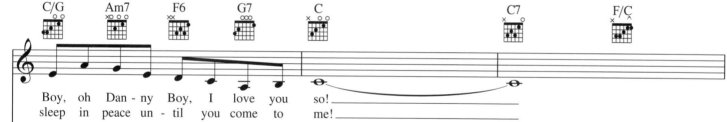

But if ye

DEAR LITTLE SHAMROCK

Traditional Irish Folksong

There's a dear lit-tle plant that grows in our
That ___ dear lit-tle plant still grows in our
That ___ dear lit-tle plant that springs from our

isle. 'Twas Saint Pat-rick him-self sure that set it.
land, fresh and fair as the daugh-ters of Er-in,
soil, when its three lit-tle leaves are ex-tend-ed,

And the sun on his la-bour with pleas-ure did
whose ___ smiles can be-witch, and with whose eyes can did
de-notes from the witch, we to-geth-er should

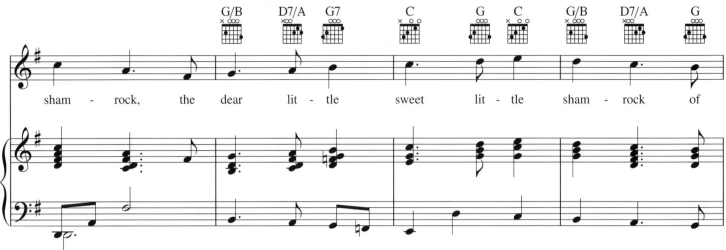

sham - rock, the dear lit - tle sweet lit - tle sham - rock of

Ire - land. The dear lit - tle sham - rock, the sweet lit - tle

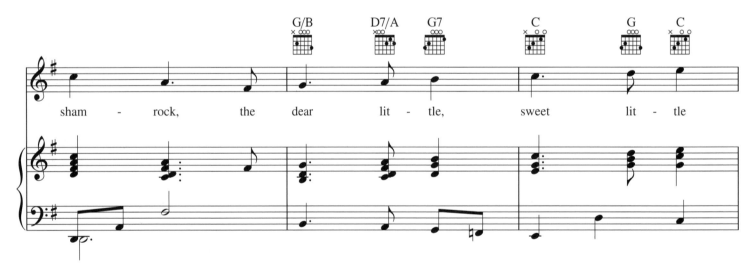

sham - rock, the dear lit - tle, sweet lit - tle

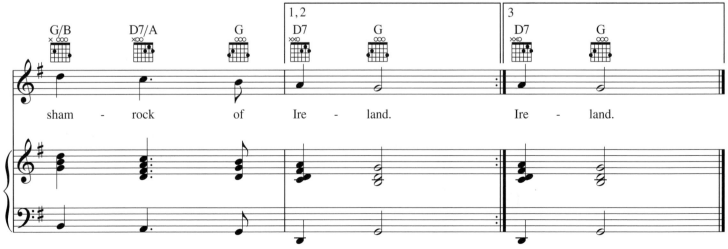

sham - rock of Ire - land. Ire - land.

FATHER O'FLYNN

Traditional Irish Folksong
Words by ALFRED P. GRAVES

Of priests we can of-fer a charm-in' va-ri-e-ty, far re-nowned_ for larn-in' and pi-e-ty. Still, I'd ad-vance ye wid-out im-pro-pri-e-ty, Fa-ther O'-Flynn as the flow'r of them all. Here's a health to you, Fa-ther O'-Flynn, *slain-té* and *slain-té* and

* pronounced "slawntia," meaning "your health"

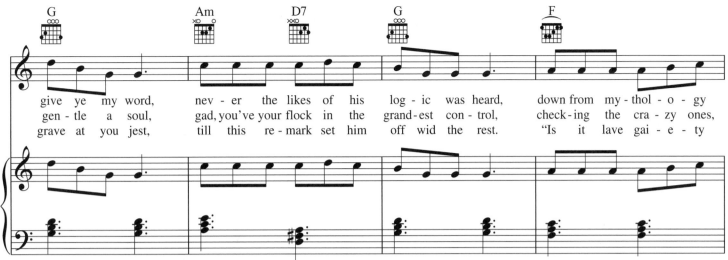

give ye my word, nev-er the likes of his log-ic was heard, down from my-thol-o-gy
gen-tle a soul, gad, you've your flock in the grand-est con-trol, check-ing the cra-zy ones,
grave at you jest, till this re-mark set him off wid the rest. "Is it lave gai-e-ty

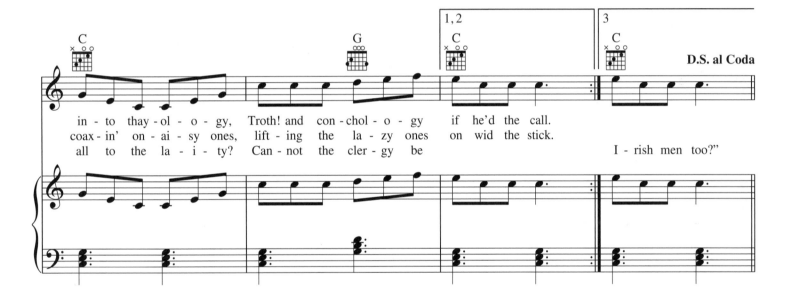

in-to thay-ol-o-gy, Troth! and con-chol-o-gy if he'd the call.
coax-in' on-ai-sy ones, lift-ing the la-zy ones on wid the stick.
all to the la-i-ty? Can-not the cler-gy be

I-rish men too?"

D.S. al Coda

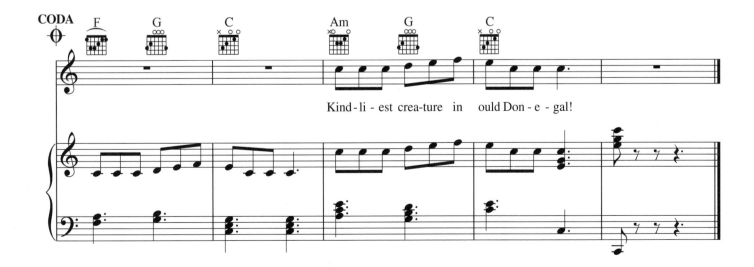

CODA

Kind-li-est crea-ture in ould Don-e-gal!

EILEEN AROON

Words by GERALD GRIFFIN
Music by LADY CAROLINE KEPPEL

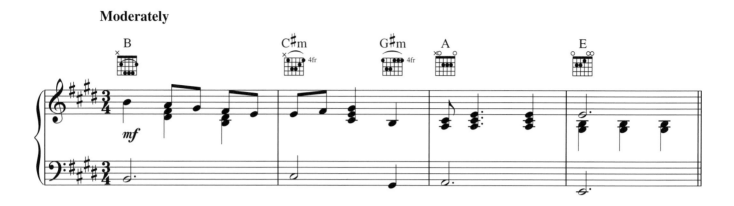

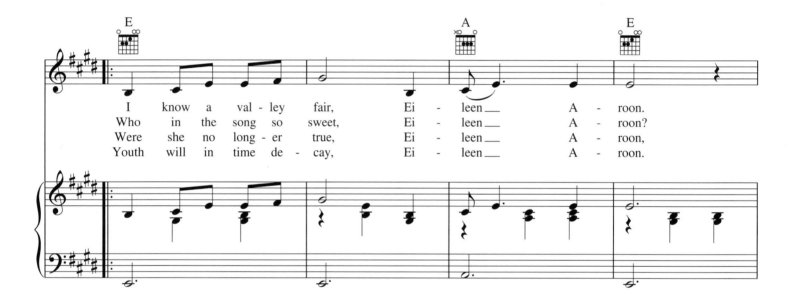

I know a val - ley fair, Ei - leen ___ A - roon.
Who in the song so sweet, Ei - leen ___ A - roon?
Were she no long - er true, Ei - leen ___ A - roon,
Youth will in time de - cay, Ei - leen ___ A - roon.

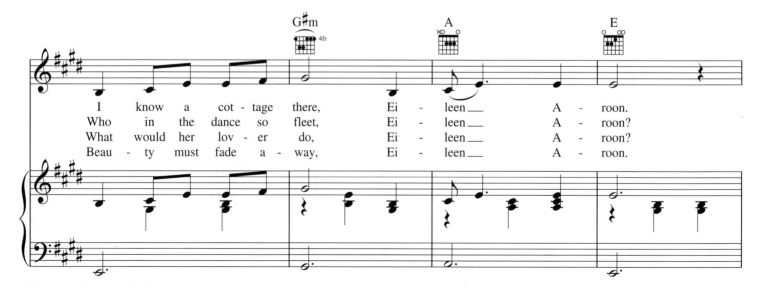

I know a cot - tage there, Ei - leen ___ A - roon.
Who in the dance so fleet, Ei - leen ___ A - roon?
What would her lov - er do, Ei - leen ___ A - roon?
Beau - ty must fade a - way, Ei - leen ___ A - roon.

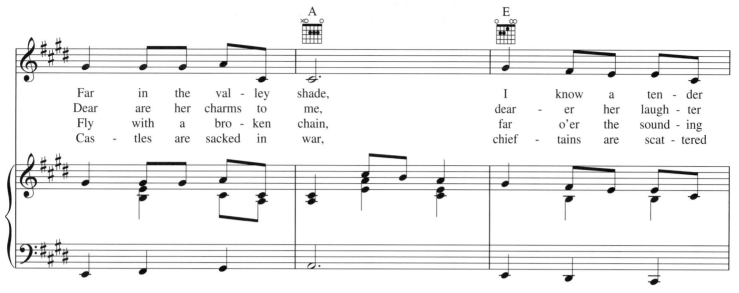

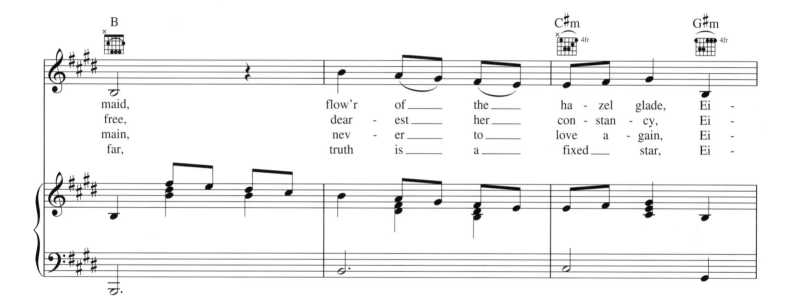

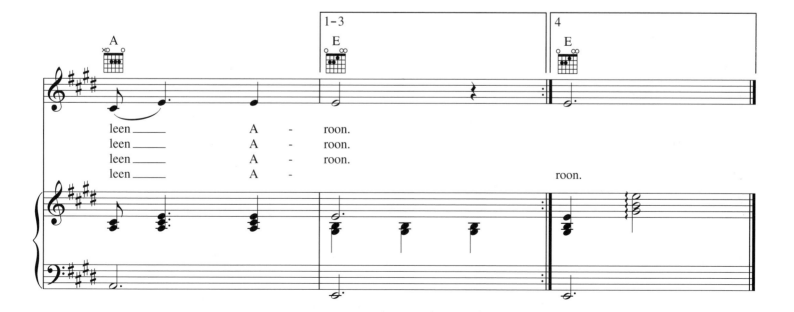

ERIN! OH ERIN!

Irish Popular Song
Words by THOMAS MOORE

45

FINNEGAN'S WAKE

Traditional Irish Folksong

Moderately

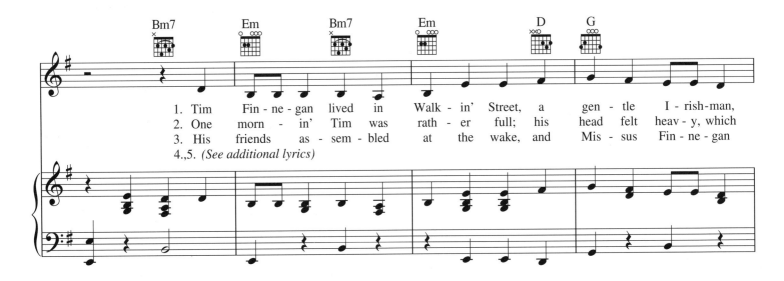

1. Tim Fin - ne - gan lived in Walk - in' Street, a gen - tle I - rish-man,
2. One morn - in' Tim was rath - er full; his head felt heav - y, which
3. His friends as - sem - bled at the wake, and Mis - sus Fin - ne - gan
4.,5. *(See additional lyrics)*

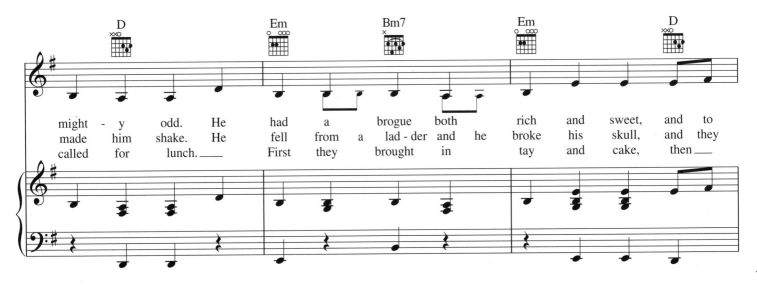

might - y odd. He had a brogue both rich and sweet, and to
made him shake. He fell from a lad - der and he broke his skull, and they
called for lunch.___ First they brought in tay and cake, then ___

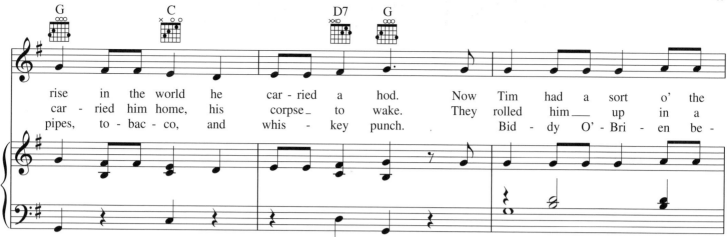

rise in the world he car - ried a hod.
car - ried him home, his corpse to wake.
pipes, to - bac - co, and whis - key punch.

Now Tim had a sort o' the
They rolled him up in a
Bid - dy O' - Bri - en be -

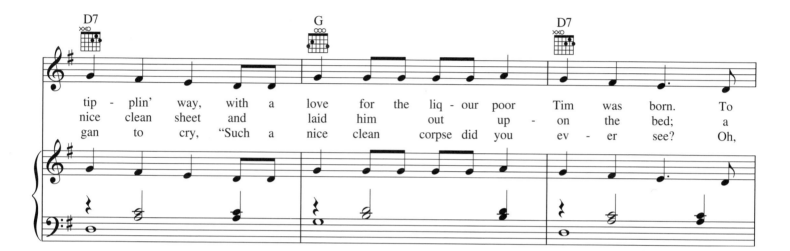

tip - plin' way, with a love for the liq - our poor Tim was born. To
nice clean sheet and laid him out up - on the bed; a
gan to cry, "Such a nice clean corpse did you ev - er see? Oh,

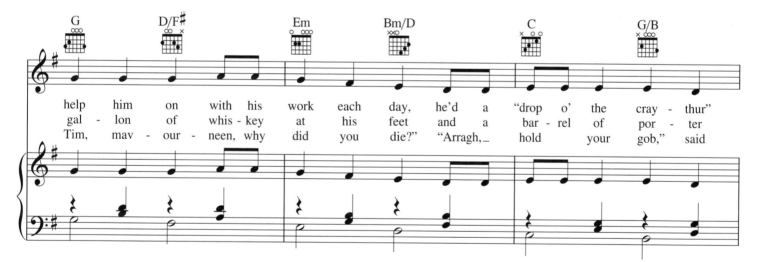

help him on with his work each day, he'd a "drop o' the cray - thur"
gal - lon of whis - key at his feet and a bar - rel of por - ter
Tim, mav - our - neen, why did you die?" "Arragh, hold your gob," said

Chorus

ev' - 'ry morn.
at his head.
Pad - dy Mc - Ghee.

Whack fol the darn O, dance to your part - ner.

Whirl the floor, your trot - ters shake; was - n't it the truth I told you? Lots of fun at Fin - ne - gan's wake.

Additional Lyrics

4. Then Maggie O'Connor took up the job,
   "Oh Biddy," says she, "you're wrong, I'm sure."
   Biddy, she gave her a belt in the gob
   And left her sprawlin' on the floor.
   And then the war did soon engage,
   'Twas woman to woman and man to man.
   Shillelaigh law was all the rage,
   And a row and ruction soon began.
   Chorus

5. Then Mickey Maloney ducked his head
   When a noggin of whiskey flew at him.
   It missed, and falling on the bed,
   The liquor scattered over Tim!
   The corpse revives; see how he rises!
   Timothy, rising from the bed,
   Said, "Whirl your whiskey around like blazes,
   Thanum an Dhul! Do you think I'm dead?"
   Chorus

GREEN GROWS THE LAUREL

Traditional Irish Folksong

see,   But I'll soon find an - oth - er far bet - ter than
kill;   Though he hates and de - tests me, I love that lad
mine;   You write to your love and I'll write to
know   That the men are de - ceiv - ers wher - ev - er they

he.
still.
mine.
go.

Green   grows the lau - rel and

soft   falls the dew;   sor - ry was I,_____ love,

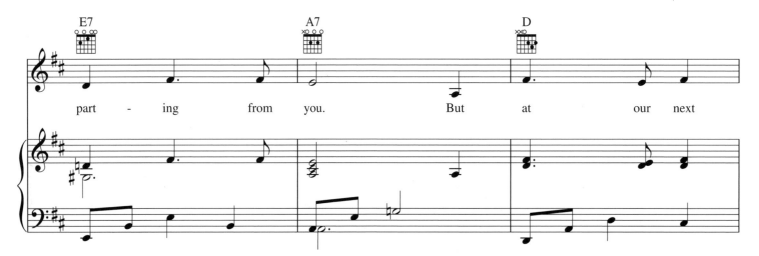

part - ing from you.   But at our next

meet - ing   I   hope   you'll   prove   true,   And   we'll   join   the   green

lau - rel   and   the   vio - let   so   blue.

rit.   *a tempo*

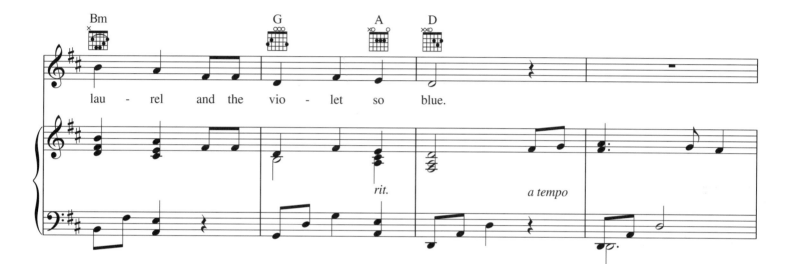

He
I
Now I

THE FOGGY DEW

Traditional Irish Folksong

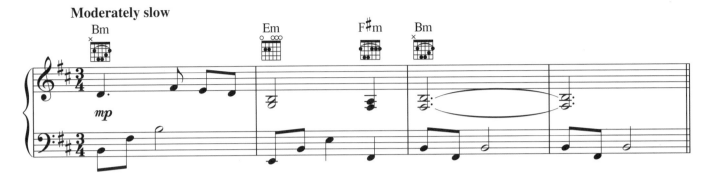

O - ver the hills I ____ went one day; a ____ love - ly ____
O - ver the hills I ____ went one morn, a - sing - ing ____

maid I spied. ____ With her coal - black ____ hair and her
I did go. ____ Met this love - ly ____ maid with her

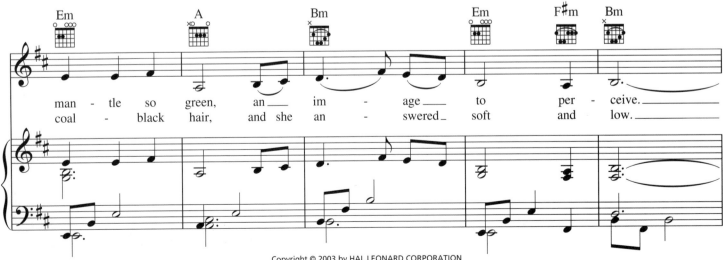

man - tle so green, an ____ im - age ____ to per - ceive. ____
coal - black hair, and she an - swered ____ soft and low. ____

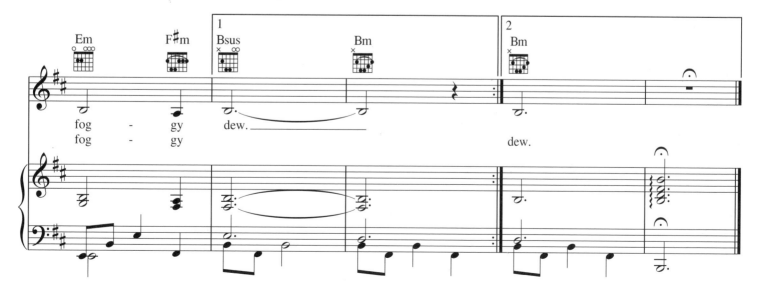

GARRYOWEN

Traditional Irish Folksong

stead of spa we'll drink down ale and __ pay the reck - 'ning

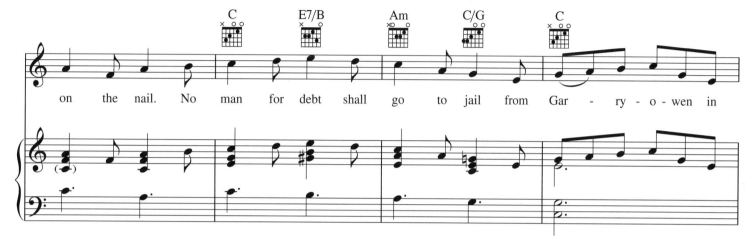

on the nail. No man for debt shall go to jail from Gar - ry - o - wen in

glo - ry. glo - ry.

Additional Lyrics

4. We'll beat the bailiffs out of fun,
   We'll make the mayors and sheriffs run.
   We are the boys no man dares dun,
   If he regards a whole skin.
   Chorus

5. Our hearts so stout have got us fame,
   For soon 'tis known from whence we came.
   Where'er we go they dread the name
   Of Garryowen in glory.
   Chorus

GIRL I LEFT BEHIND ME

Traditional Irish Folksong

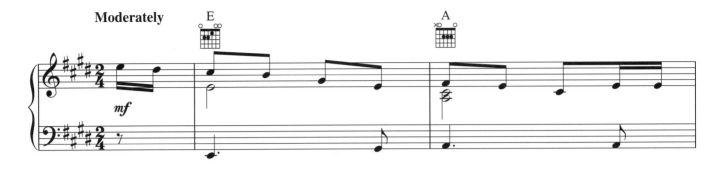

I'm ___ lone - some since I
ne'er shall since I for -

cross'd the hill, and o'er the moor ___ and ___ val - ley. Such
get the night and the stars were bright ___ a - bove me, and ___

heav - y thoughts my heart do fill since part - ing with my ___
gen - tly lent their sil - v'ry light since when first she vow'd she ___

Sal - ly. I _____ seek no more the fine and gay, for
loved me. But _____ now I'm bound to Brigh - ton Camp, kind

each does but re - mind me how _____ swift the hours did
heav'n may fa - vor find me, and _____ send me safe - ly

pass a - way with the girl I left be - hind me.
back a - gain to the girl I left be -

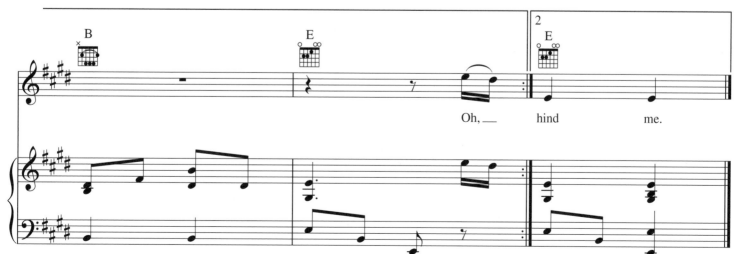

Oh, _____ hind me.

HARRIGAN
from GEORGE M!

Words and Music by
GEORGE M. COHAN

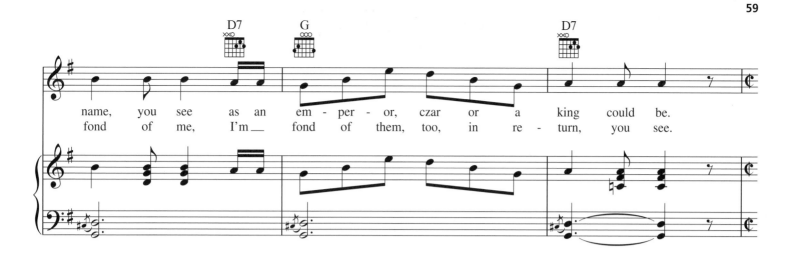

name, you see as an em-per-or, czar or a king could be.
fond of me, I'm— fond of them, too, in re-turn, you see.

Who is the man helps a man ev-'ry time he can? Har-ri-gan, that's
Who is the gent that's de-serv-ing a mon-u-ment? Har-ri-gan, that's

me! _____ }
me! _____ }

H - A - dou-ble R - I -

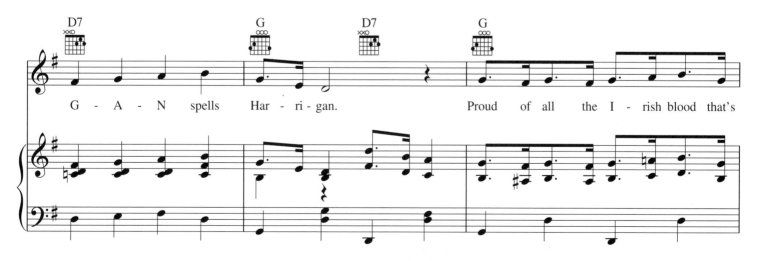

G - A - N spells Har-ri-gan. Proud of all the I - rish blood that's

I'LL TAKE YOU HOME AGAIN, KATHLEEN

Words and Music by
THOMAS WESTENDORF

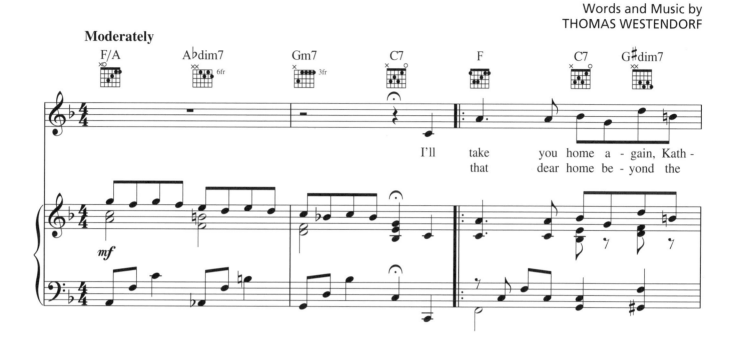

I'll take you home a - gain, Kath -
that dear home be - yond the

leen, A - cross the o - cean wild and wide, To
sea My Kath - leen shall a - gain re - turn And

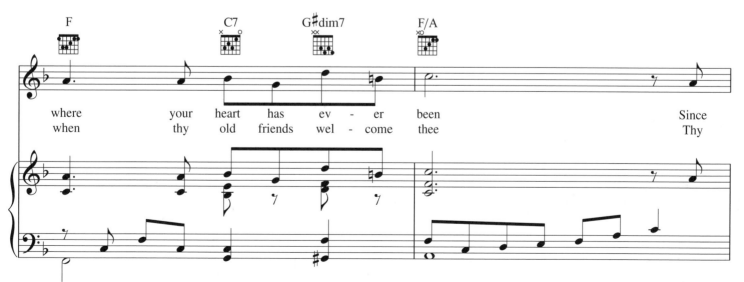

where your heart has ev - er been Since
when thy old friends wel - come thee Thy

tears   be - dim your lov - ing eyes.
all   your grief will be for - got.   Oh,

I   will take you back, Kath - leen,   To where   your heart will feel no

pain.   And when   the fields are fresh and green   I'll ___

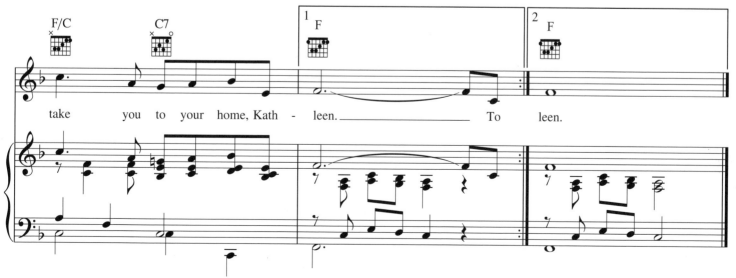

take   you to your home, Kath - leen. _____ To   leen.

HAS SORROW THY YOUNG DAYS SHADED?

Traditional Irish Folksong

Moderately slow

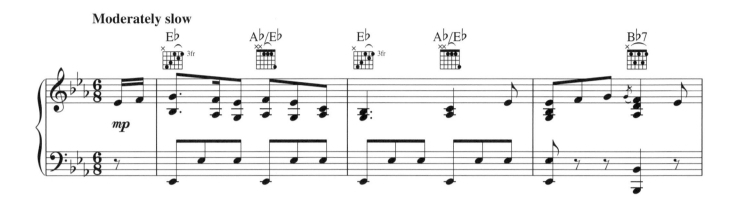

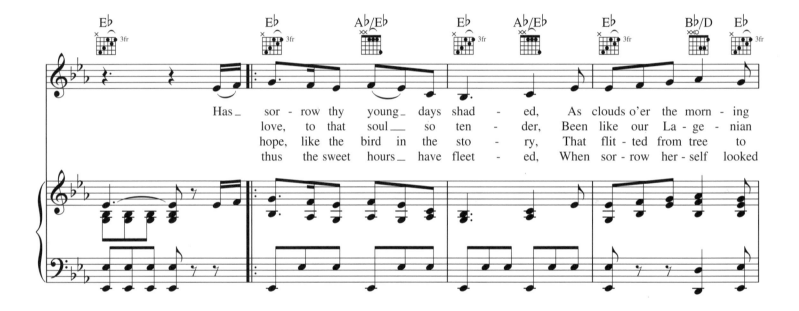

Has _ sor - row thy young _ days shad - ed, As clouds o'er the morn - ing
love, to that soul _ so ten - der, Been like our La - ge - nian
hope, like the bird in the sto - ry, That flit - ted from tree to
thus the sweet hours _ have fleet - ed, When sor - row her - self looked

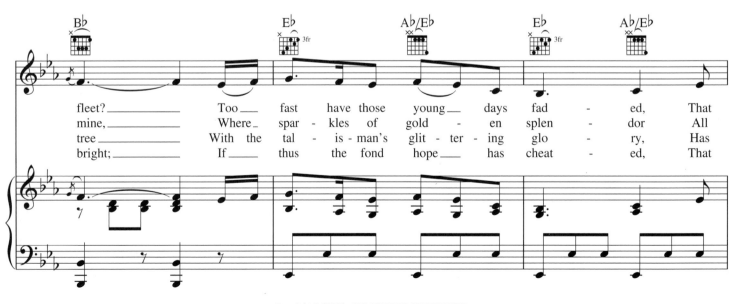

fleet? _____ Too _ fast have those young _ days fad - ed, That
mine, _____ Where _ spar - kles of gold - en splen - dor All
tree _____ With the tal - is - man's glit - ter - ing glo - ry, Has
bright; _____ If _ thus the fond hope _ has cheat - ed, That

HUNTING THE HARE

Traditional Irish Folksong

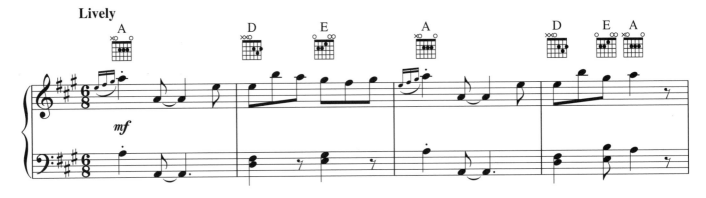

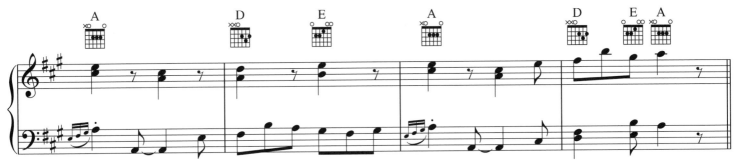

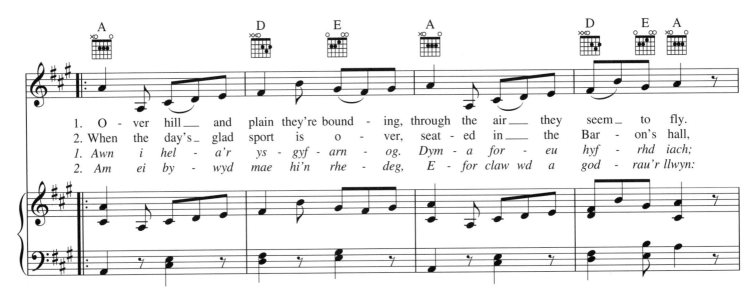

1. O - ver hill ___ and plain they're bound - ing, through the air ___ they seem ___ to fly.
2. When the day's ___ glad sport is o - ver, seat - ed in ___ the Bar - on's hall,
1. Awn i hel - a'r ys - gyf - arn - og. Dym - a for - eu hyf - rhd iach;
2. Am ei by - wyd mae hi'n rhe - deg, E - for claw d a god - rau'r llwyn:

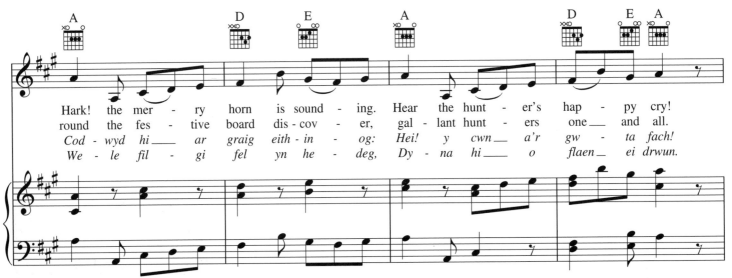

Hark! the mer - ry horn is sound - ing. Hear the hunt - er's hap - py cry!
round the fes - tive board dis - cov - er, gal - lant hunt - ers one ___ and all.
Cod - wyd hi ___ ar graig eith - in - og: Hei! y cwn ___ a'r gw - ta fach!
We - le fil - gi fel yn he - deg, Dy - na hi ___ o flaen ___ ei drwun.

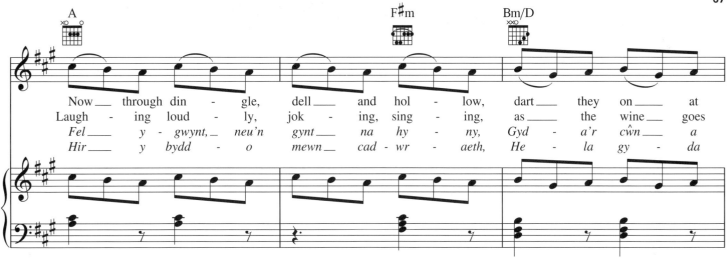

Now__ through din - gle, dell __ and hol - low, dart __ they on __ at
Laugh - ing loud - ly, jok - ing, sing - ing, as __ the wine __ goes
Fel __ y - gwynt,_ neu'n gynt __ na hy - ny, Gyd - a'r cŵn __ a
Hir __ y bydd - o mewn __ cad - wr - aeth, He - la gy - da

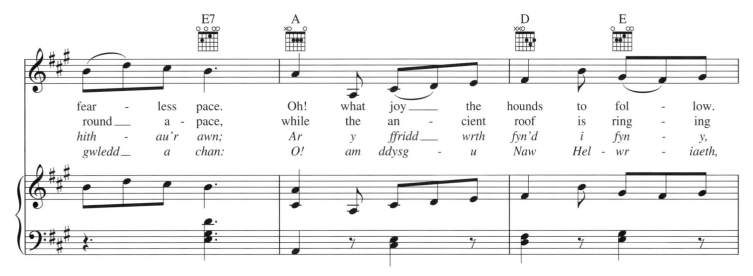

fear - less pace. Oh! what joy __ the hounds to fol - low.
round __ a - pace, while the an - cient roof is ring - ing
hith - au'r awn; Ar y ffridd __ wrth fyn'd i fyn - y,
gwledd_ a chan: O! am ddysg - u Naw Hel - wr - iaeth,

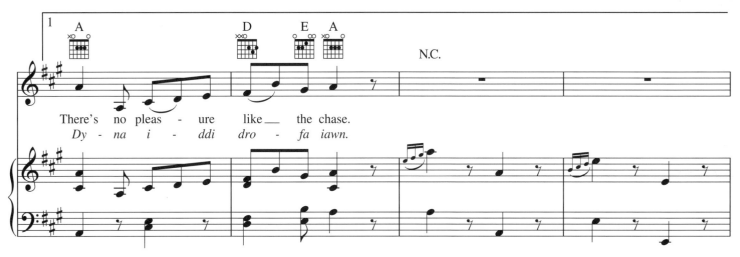

1

There's no pleas - ure like __ the chase.
Dy - na i - ddi dro - fa iawn.

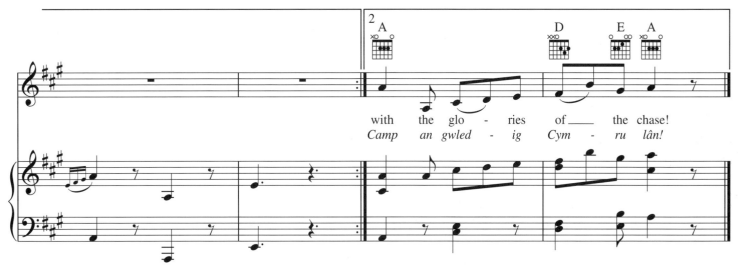

2

with the glo - ries of __ the chase!
Camp an gwled - ig Cym - ru lân!

I'LL TELL ME MA

Traditional Irish Folksong

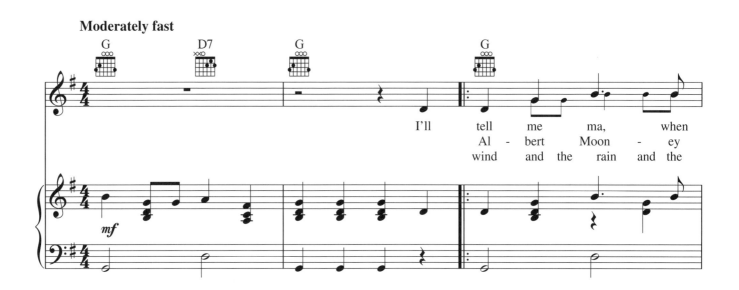

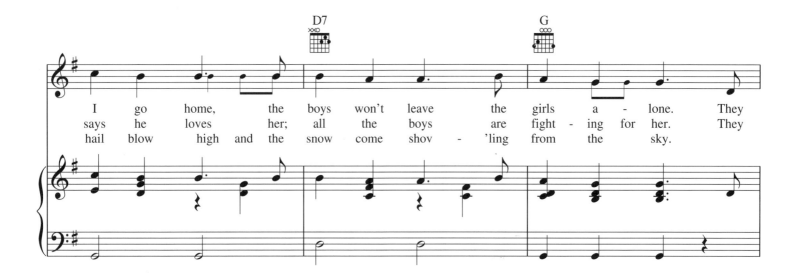

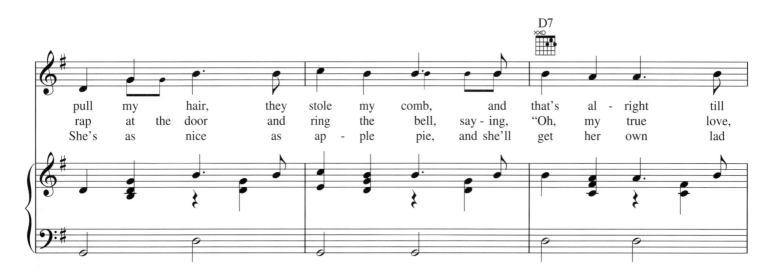

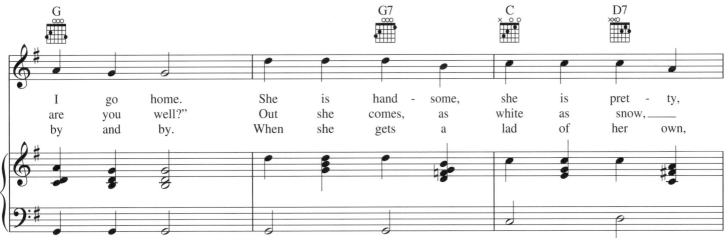

I go home. She is hand-some, she is pret-ty,
are you well?" Out she comes, as white as snow,_____
by and by. When she gets a lad of her own,

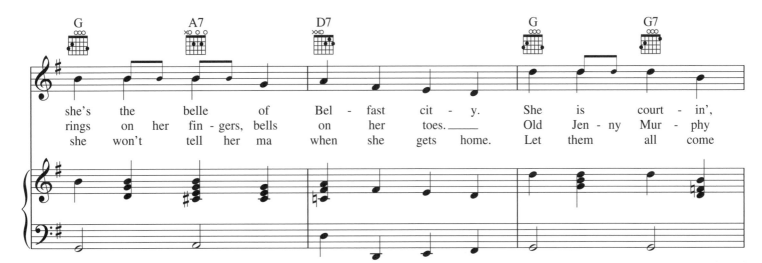

she's the belle of Bel-fast cit-y. She is court-in',
rings on her fin-gers, bells on her toes._____ Old Jen-ny Mur-phy
she won't tell her ma when she gets home. Let them all come

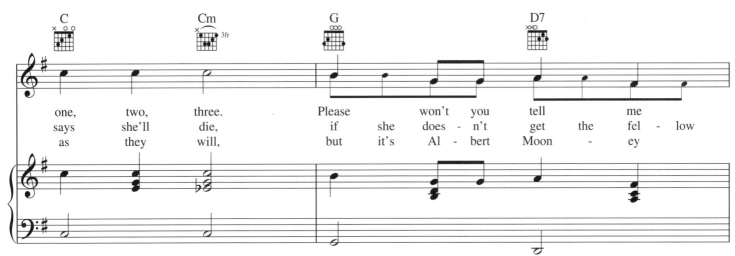

one, two, three. Please won't you tell me
says she'll die, if she does-n't get the fel-low
as they will, but it's Al-bert Moon-ey

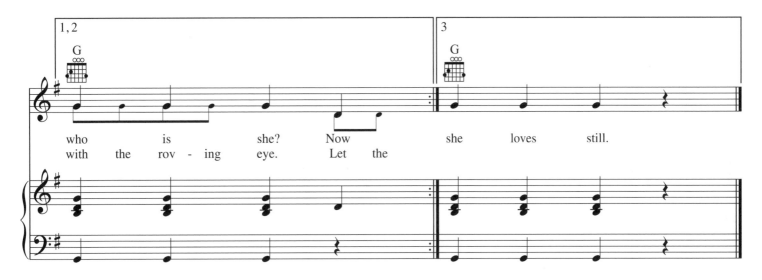

who is she? Now she loves still.
with the rov-ing eye. Let the

I'M A ROVER AND SELDOM SOBER

Traditional Irish Folksong

I'm a rov - er and sel - dom so - ber, I'm a rov - er o' high de - gree. It's when I'm drink - ing I'm al - ways think - ing how to gain my love's com - pa - ny.

1. Though the night be as dark as
2. He step - pit up to her bed - room
3. She raised her heid on her snaw - white
4.-7. *(See additional lyrics)*

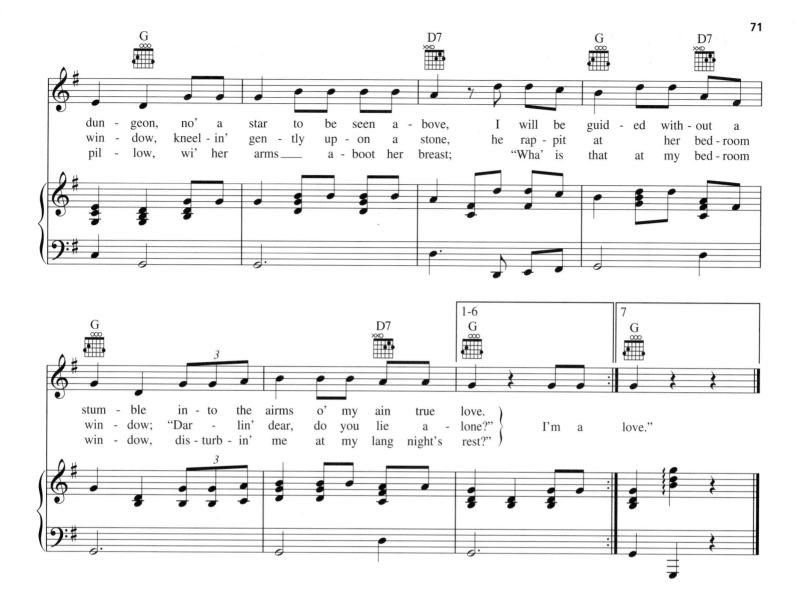

G   **D7**   **G**   **D7**

dun - geon, no' a star to be seen a - bove, I will be guid - ed with - out a

win - dow, kneel - in' gen - tly up - on a stone, he rap - pit at her bed - room

pil - low, wi' her arms___ a - boot her breast; "Wha' is that at my bed - room

G   **D7**   **1-6** **G**   **7** **G**

stum - ble in - to the airms o' my ain true love.

win - dow; "Dar - lin' dear, do you lie a - lone?"   I'm a love."

win - dow, dis - turb - in' me at my lang night's rest?"

Additional Lyrics

4. "It's only me, your ain true lover;
   Open the door and let me in,
   For I hae come on a lang journey
   And I'm near drenched to the skin."

5. She opened the door wi' the greatest pleasure,
   She opened the door and she let him in;
   They baith shook hands and embraced each other,
   Until the mornin' they lay as one.

6. The cocks were crawin', the birds were whistlin',
   The burns they ran free abune the brae;
   "Remember, lass, I'm a ploughman laddie
   And the fairmer I must obey."

7. "Noo, my lass, I must gang and leave thee,
   And though the hills they are high above,
   I will climb them wi' greater pleasure
   Since I been in the airms o' my love."

IRELAND MUST BE HEAVEN, FOR MY MOTHER CAME FROM THERE

Words by JOSEPH McCARTHY
and HOWARD JOHNSON
Music by FRED FISHER

Moderately

I've

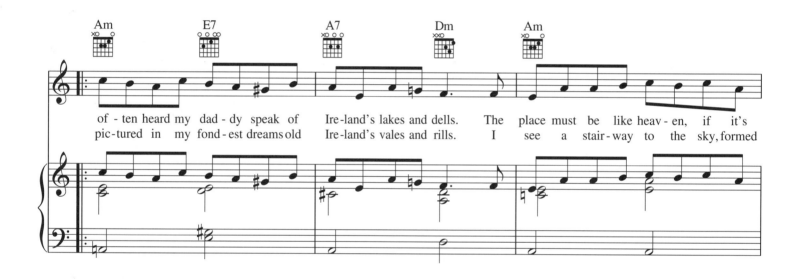

of - ten heard my dad - dy speak of Ire - land's lakes and dells. The place must be like heav - en, if it's
pic - tured in my fond - est dreams old Ire - land's vales and rills. I see a stair - way to the sky, formed

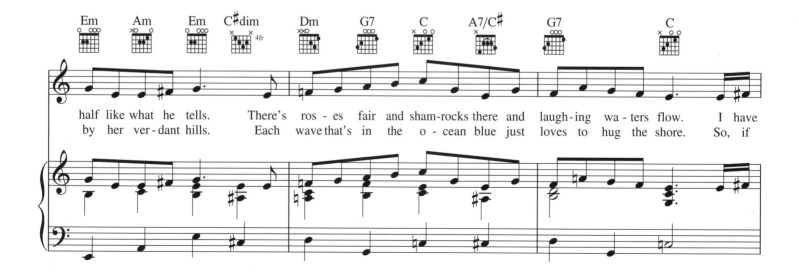

half like what he tells. There's ros - es fair and sham - rocks there and laugh - ing wa - ters flow. I have
by her ver - dant hills. Each wave that's in the o - cean blue just loves to hug the shore. So, if

THE IRISH ROVER

Traditional Irish Folksong

In the

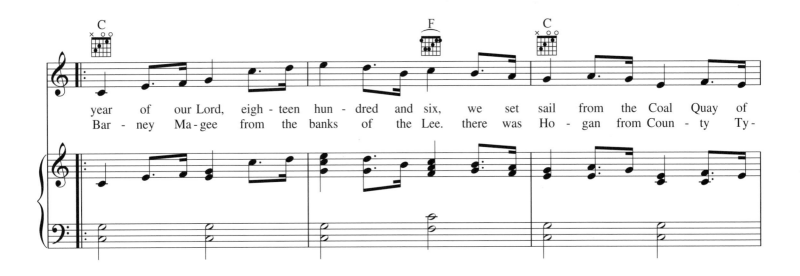

year of our Lord, eigh-teen hun-dred and six, we set sail from the Coal Quay of
Bar-ney Ma-gee from the banks of the Lee. there was Ho-gan from Coun-ty Ty-

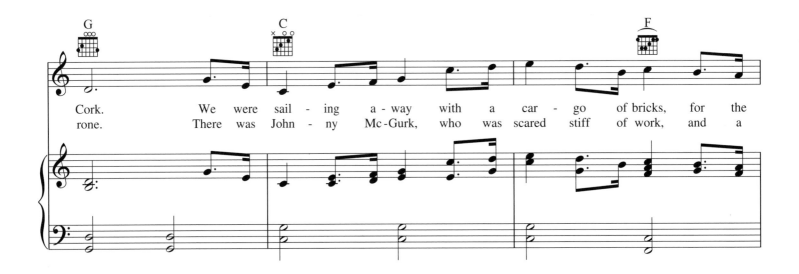

Cork. We were sail-ing a-way with a car-go of bricks, for the
rone. There was John-ny Mc-Gurk, who was scared stiff of work, and a

grand cit - y hall in New York. We'd an el - e - gant craft, it was
chap from West-meath named Ma - lone. There was Slug - ger O' - Toole, who was

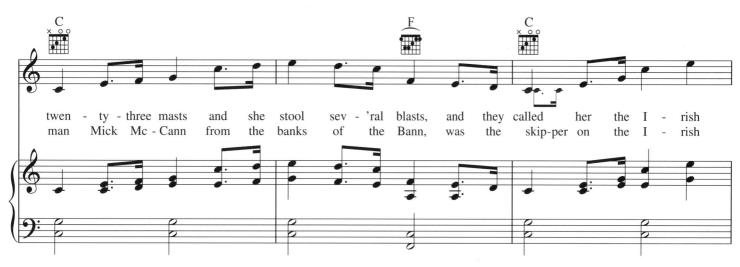

rigged fore and aft, and how_____ the trade winds drove_____ her. She had
drunk as a rule, and fight - ing Bill Tra - cy from Do - ver. And your

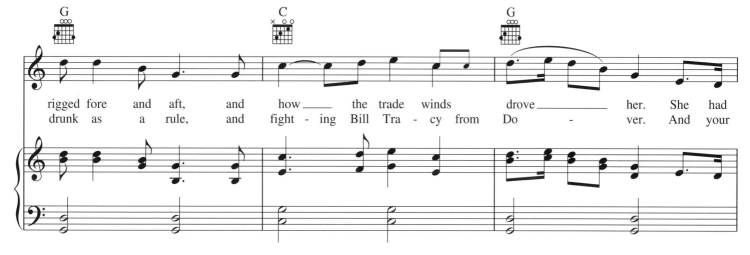

twen - ty - three masts and she stool sev - 'ral blasts, and they called her the I - rish
man Mick Mc - Cann from the banks of the Bann, was the skip - per on the I - rish

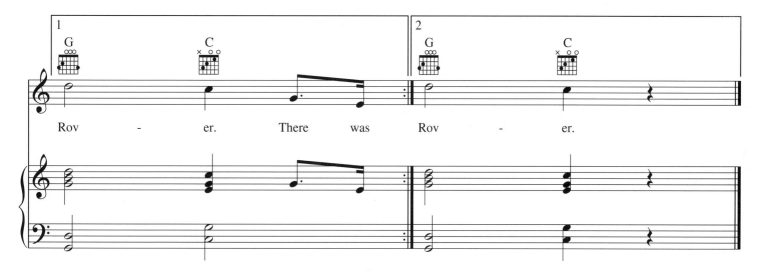

Rov - er. There was Rov - er.

THE IRISH WASHERWOMAN

Traditional Irish Folksong

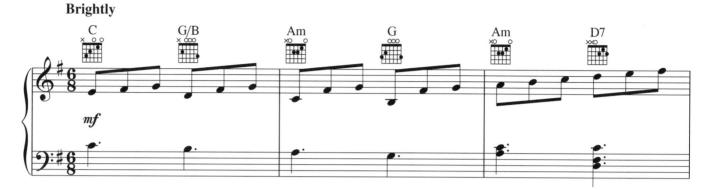

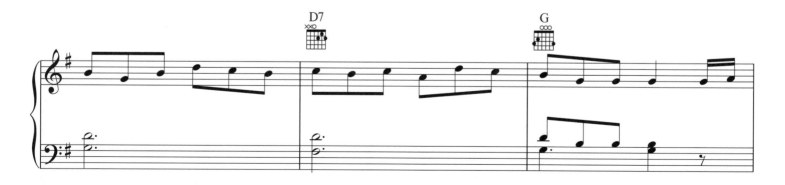

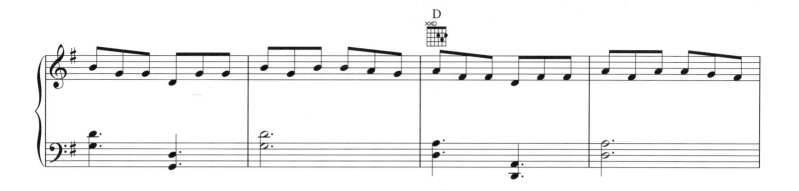

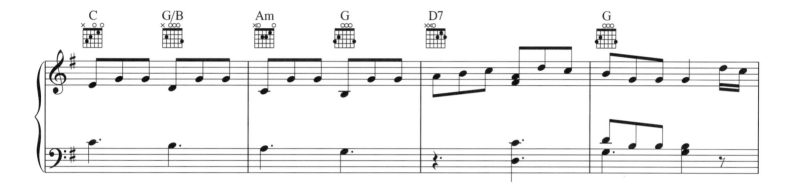

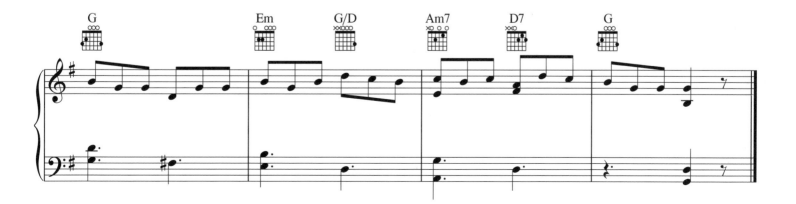

JUG OF PUNCH

Traditional Irish Folksong

'Twas ver - y

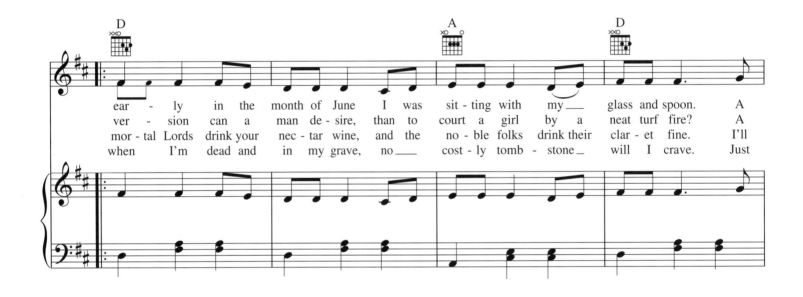

ear - ly in the month of June I was sit - ting with my___ glass and spoon. A
ver - sion can a man de - sire, than to court a girl by a neat turf fire? A
mor - tal Lords drink your nec - tar wine, and the no - ble folks drink their clar - et fine. I'll
when I'm dead and in my grave, no___ cost - ly tomb - stone___ will I crave. Just

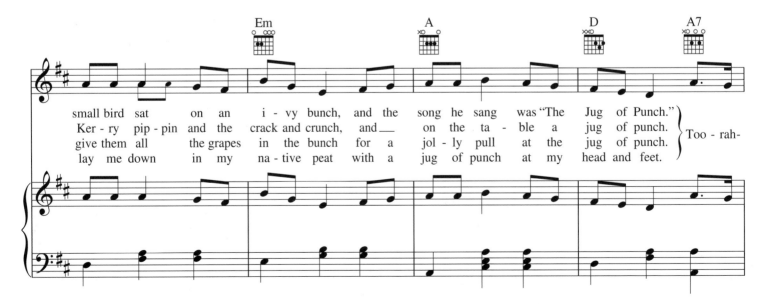

small bird sat on an i - vy bunch, and the song he sang was "The Jug of Punch."
Ker - ry pip - pin and the crack and crunch, and___ on the ta - ble a jug of punch.
give them all the grapes in the bunch for a jol - ly pull at the jug of punch.
lay me down in my na - tive peat with a jug of punch at my head and feet.

Too - rah-

loo - rah - loo, too - rah - loo - rah lay. Too - rah - loo - rah - loo, too - rah - loo - rah lay.

A
A
I'll
Just

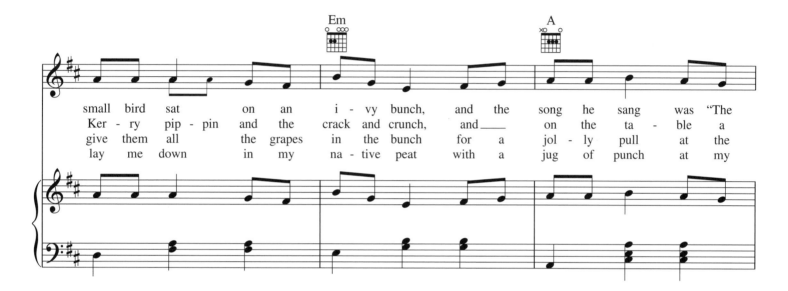

small bird sat on an i - vy bunch, and the song he sang was "The
Ker - ry pip - pin and the crack and crunch, and ___ on the ta - ble a
give them all the grapes in the bunch for a jol - ly pull at the
lay me down in my na - tive peat with a jug of punch at my

Jug of Punch."   What more di -   head and feet.
jug of punch.   All ye
jug of punch.   Oh, but

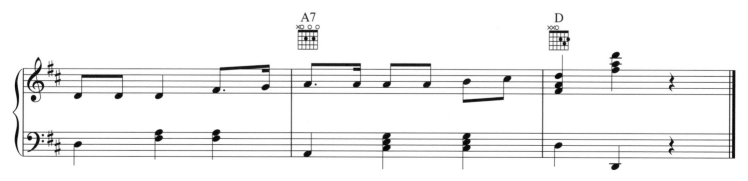

KERRY DANCE

By J.L. MOLLOY

Oh, the days of the Ker-ry danc-ing! Oh, the ring of the pip-er's tune!

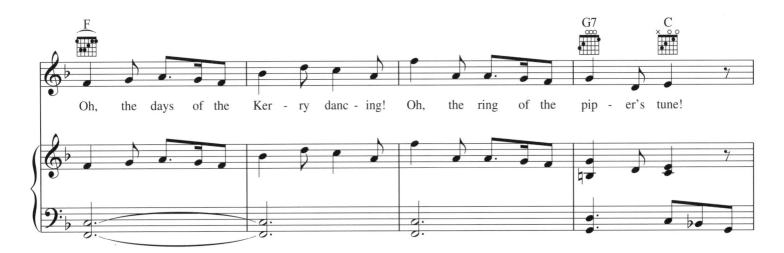

Oh, for one of those hours of glad-ness, gone, a-las, like our youth, too soon.

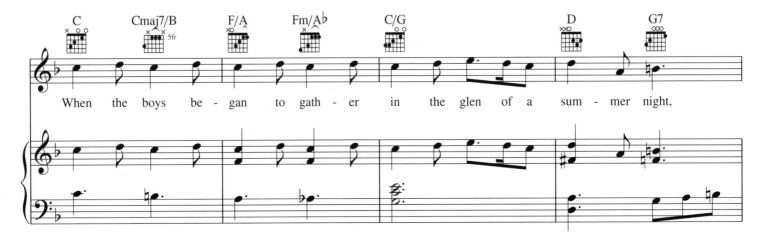

When the boys be-gan to gath-er in the glen of a sum-mer night,

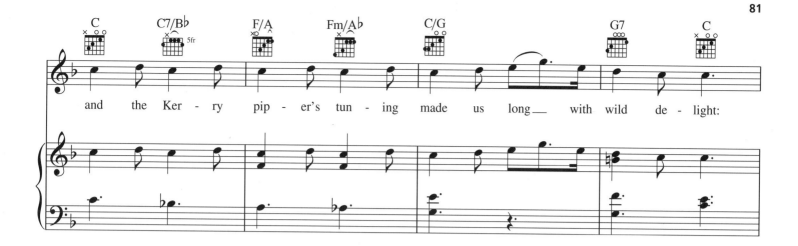

and the Ker-ry pip-er's tun-ing made us long____ with wild de-light:

Oh, to think of it! Oh, to dream of it fills my heart with tears.

Oh, the days of the Ker-ry danc-ing! Oh, the ring of the pip-er's tune! Oh, for one of those

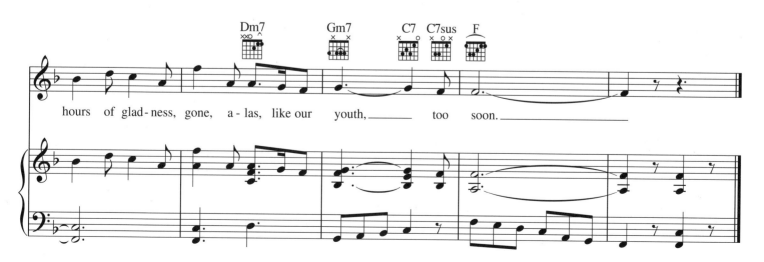

hours of glad-ness, gone, a-las, like our youth,____ too soon.____

KILLARNEY

Words and Music by
MICHAEL W. BALFE

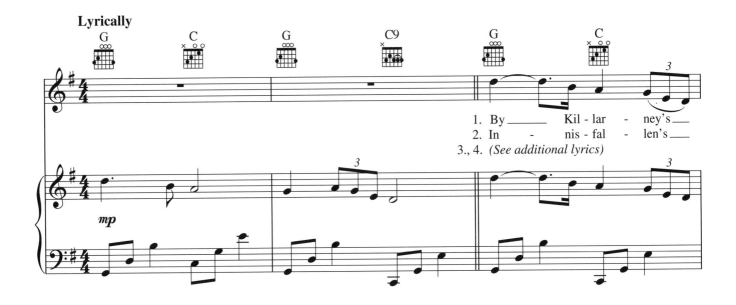

1. By _____ Kil - lar - ney's _____
2. In _____ nis - fal - len's _____
3., 4. *(See additional lyrics)*

lakes and fells, em - 'rald isles and _____ wind - ing bays,
ru - ined shrine may _____ sug - gest a _____ pass - ing sigh,

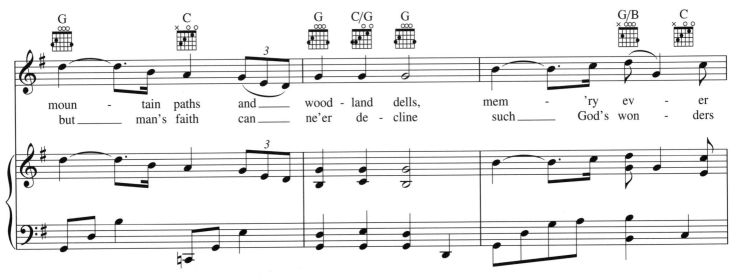

moun - tain paths and _____ wood - land dells, mem - 'ry ev - er
but _____ man's faith can _____ ne'er de - cline such _____ God's won - ders

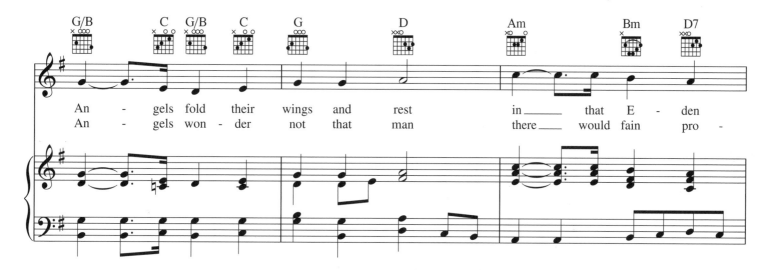

Additional Lyrics

3. No place else can charm the eye with such bright and varied tints.
   Ev'ry rock that you pass by, verdure 'broiders or besprints.
   Virgin there the green grass grows. Ev'ry morn springs natal day.
   Bright-hued berries daff the snows. Smiling winters frown away.
   Angels, often pausing there, doubt if Eden were more fair.
   Beauty's home, Killarney! Ever fair, Killarney!

4. Music there for echo dwells, makes each sound a harmony.
   Many-voiced, the chorus swells 'til it faints in ecstasy.
   With the charmful tints below, seems the Heav'n above to vie:
   All rich colors that we know tinge the cloudwreaths in that sky.
   Wings of angels so might shine, glancing back soft light divine.
   Beauty's home, Killarney! Ever fair, Killarney!

LANNIGAN'S BALL

Traditional Irish Folksong

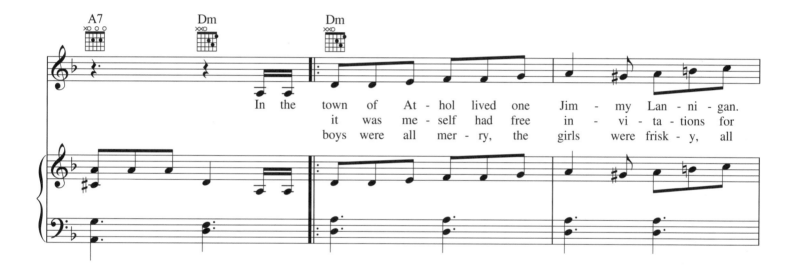

In the town of At - hol lived one Jim - my Lan - ni - gan.
it was me - self had free in - vi - ta - tions for
boys were all mer - ry, the girls were frisk - y, all

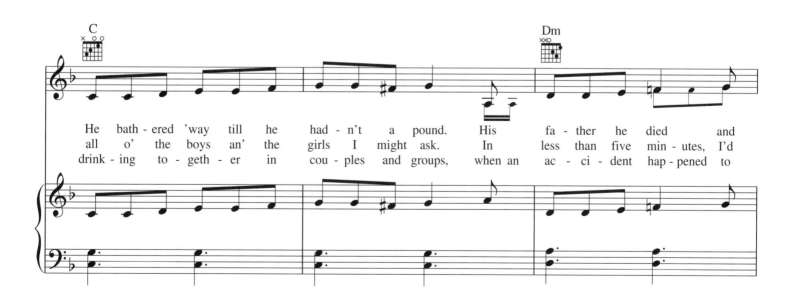

He bath - ered 'way till he had - n't a pound. His fa - ther he died and
all o' the boys an' the girls I might ask. In less than five min - utes, I'd
drink - ing to - geth - er in cou - ples and groups, when an ac - ci - dent hap - pened to

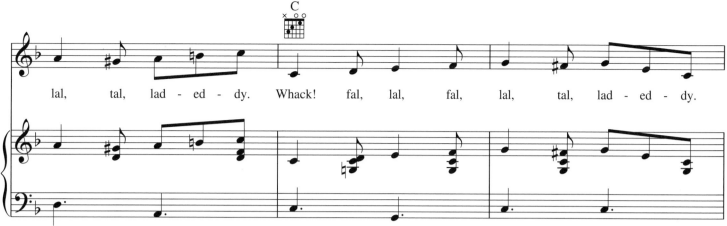

lal, tal, lad - ed - dy. Whack! fal, lal, fal, lal, tal, lad - ed - dy.

Whack! fal, lal, fal, lal, tal lad - ed - dy. Whack! hur - roo! ___ for

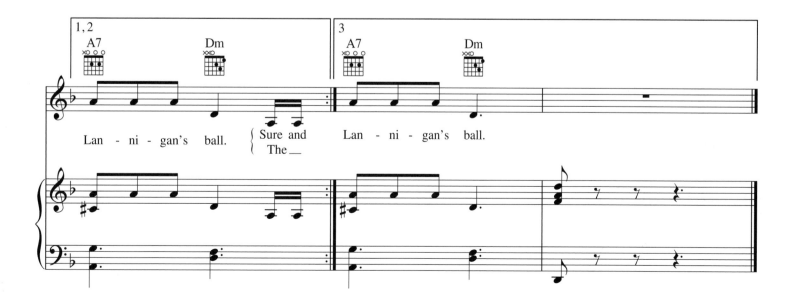

Lan - ni - gan's ball. { Sure and   Lan - ni - gan's ball.
                         The ___

LEAVING OF LIVERPOOL

Traditional Irish Sea Chantey

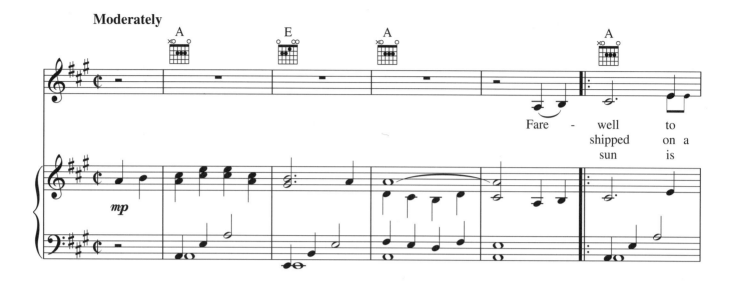

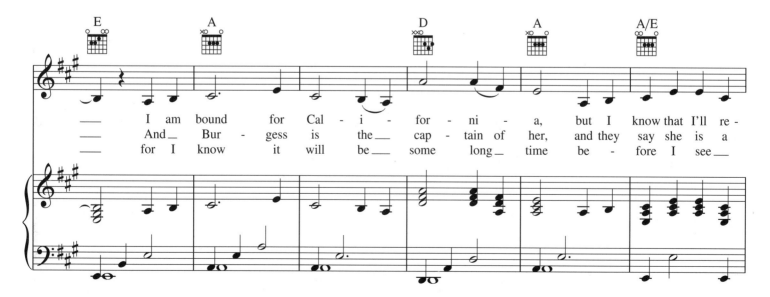

turn some day.
float - ing hell.
you a - gain.

So __ fare thee well, my __ own true

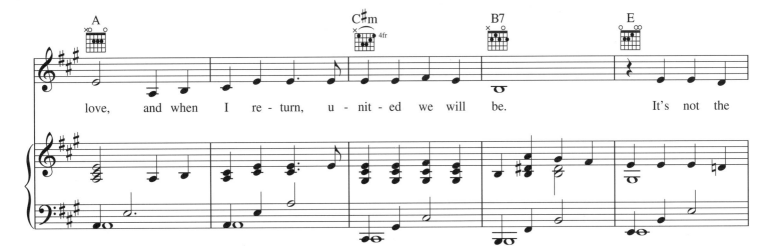

love, and when I re - turn, u - nit - ed we will be. It's not the

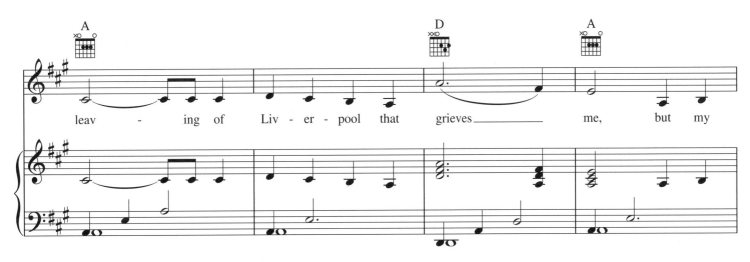

leav - ing of Liv - er - pool that grieves _____ me, but my

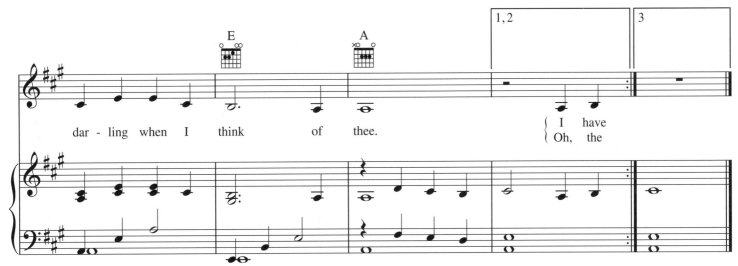

dar - ling when I think of thee.

I have
Oh, the

LET ERIN REMEMBER THE DAYS OF OLD

Words by THOMAS MOORE
Traditional Irish Folk Melody

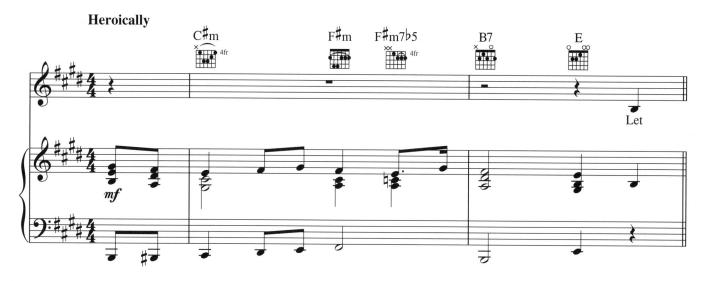

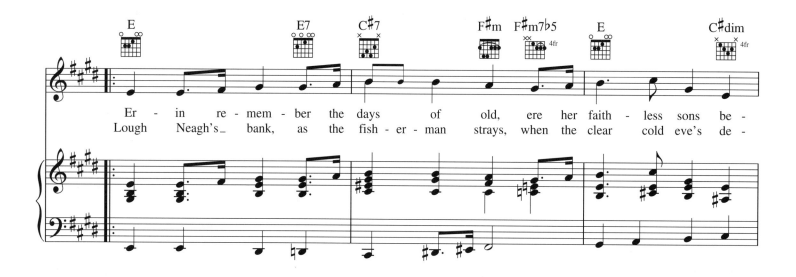

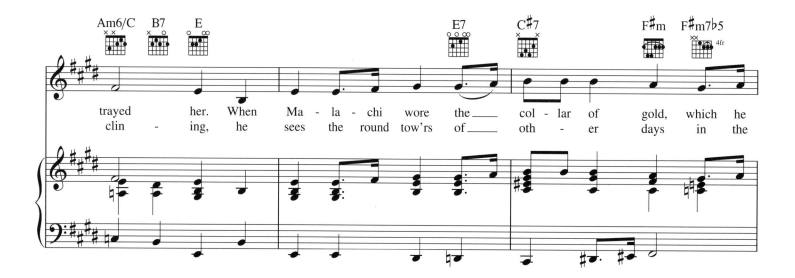

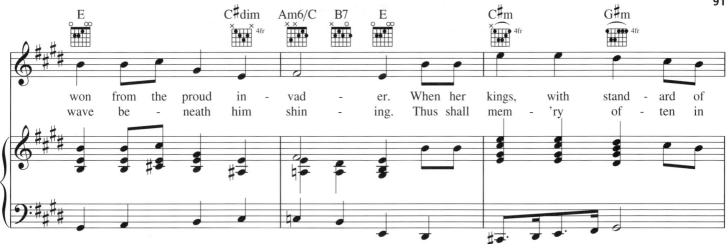

won from the proud in - vad - er. When her kings, with stand - ard of
wave be - neath him shin - ing. Thus shall mem - 'ry of - ten in

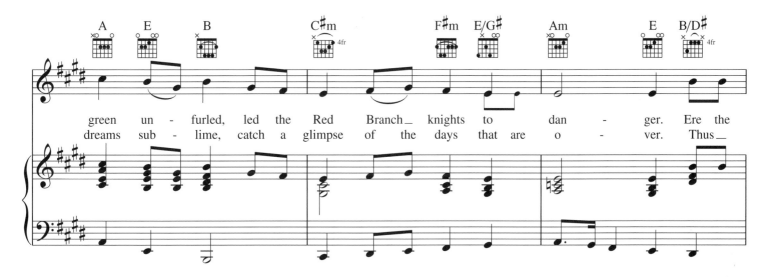

green un - furled, led the Red Branch knights to dan - ger. Ere the
dreams sub - lime, catch a glimpse of the days that are o - ver. Thus

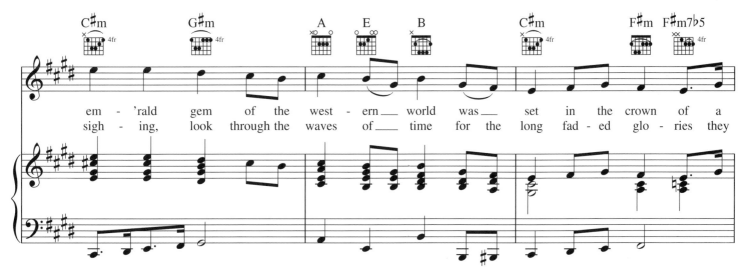

em - 'rald gem of the west - ern world was set in the crown of a
sigh - ing, look through the waves of time for the long fad - ed glo - ries they

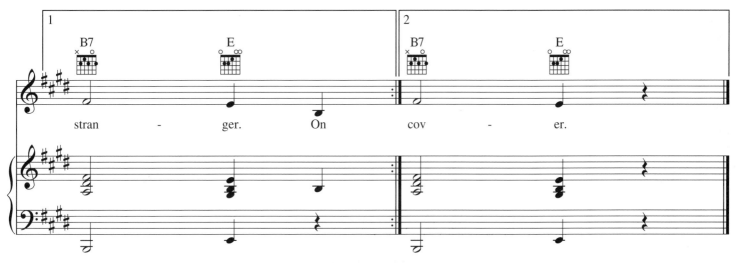

stran - ger. On cov - er.

A LITTLE BIT OF HEAVEN

Words by ERNEST R. BALL
Music by J. KEIRN BRENNAN

MACUSHLA

Words by JOSEPHINE V. ROWE
Music by DERMOT MacMURROUGH

Moderately slow

Ma -

cush - la! Ma-cush - la! Your sweet voice is call - ing, call - ing me soft - ly a -

gain and a - gain. Ma-cush - la! Ma-cush - la! I hear its dear plead - ing, my

blue - eyed Ma-cush - la, I hear it in vain. Ma - cush - la! Ma-cush - la! Your

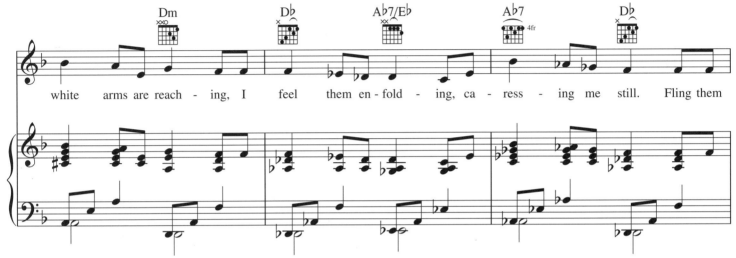

white arms are reach - ing, I feel them en-fold - ing, ca - ress - ing me still. Fling them

out from the dark - ness, my lost love, Ma-cush - la, let them

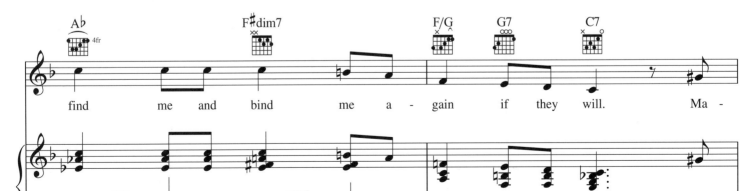

find me and bind me a - gain if they will. Ma -

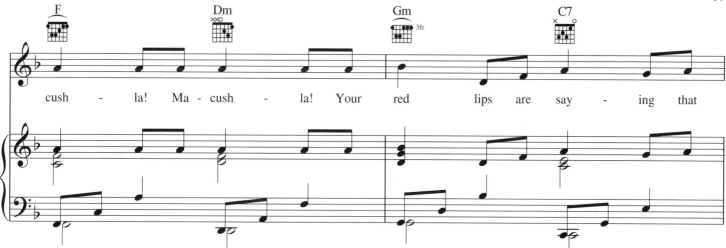

cush - la! Ma - cush - la! Your red lips are say - ing that

death is a dream and __ love is for aye. Then a - wak - en, Ma - cush - la, a -

wake __ from your dream - ing, my blue - eyed Ma - cush - la, a -

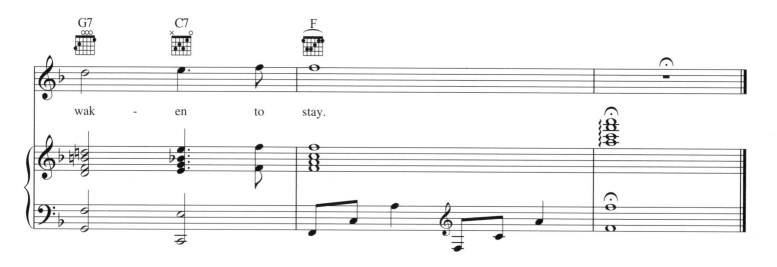

wak - en to stay.

THE LOW-BACKED CAR

Traditional Irish Folksong
Words by SAMUEL LOVER

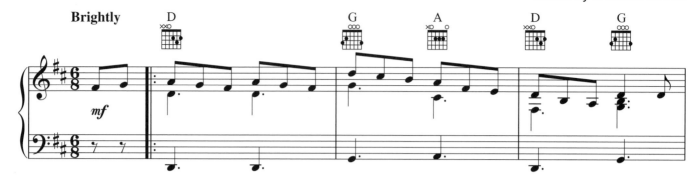

When first I saw sweet Peg - gy, 'twas on a mar - ket
In bat - tle's wild com - mo - tion, the proud and might - y
Sweet Peg - gy 'round her car, sir, has strings of ducks and

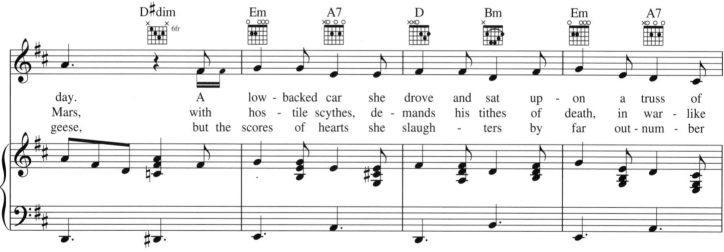

day.   A low - backed car she drove and sat up - on a truss of
Mars,   with hos - tile scythes, de - mands his tithes of death, in war - like
geese,   but the scores of hearts she slaugh - ters by far out - num - ber

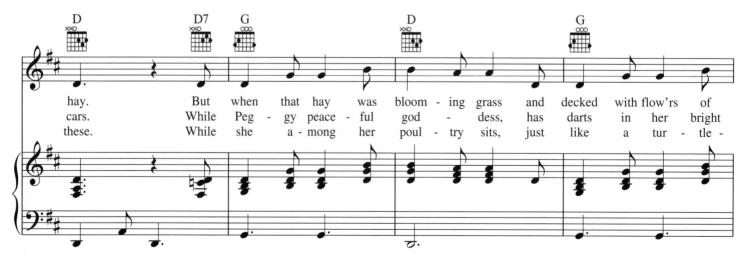

hay.   But when that hay was bloom - ing grass and decked with flow'rs of
cars.   While Peg - gy peace - ful god - dess, has darts in her bright
these.   While she a - mong her poul - try sits, just like a tur - tle -

MacNAMARA'S BAND

Words by JOHN J. STAMFORD
Music by SHAMUS O'CONNOR

March tempo

Oh! Me

name is Mac-Na-ma-ra, I'm the lead-er of the band,_____ Al-though we're few in
Now we are re-hears-in' for a ver-y swell af-fair,_____ The an-nual cel-e-

num-ber, we're the fin-est in the land. We play at wakes and wed-dings and at
bra-tion, all the gen-try will be there. When Gen-'ral Grant to Ire-land came he

ev-'ry fan-cy ball,_____ And when we play at fun-er-als we play the march from
took me by the hand,_____ Says he, "I nev-er saw the likes of Mac-Na-ma-ra's

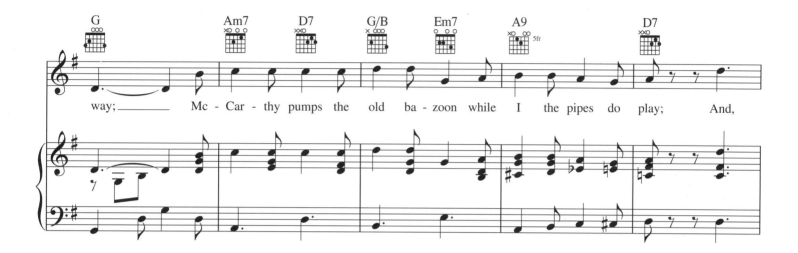

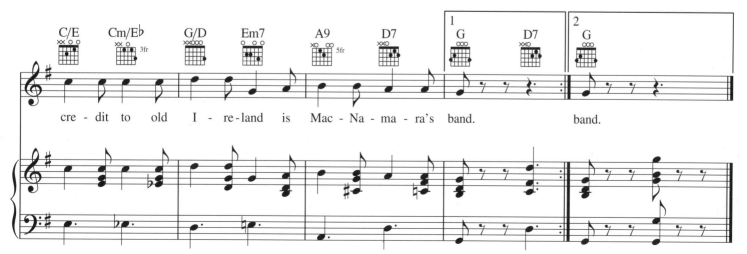

MARY'S A GRAND OLD NAME

from GEORGE M!
from FORTY-FIVE MINUTES FROM BROADWAY

Words and Music by
GEORGE M. COHAN

For it is Mar - y, Mar - y,

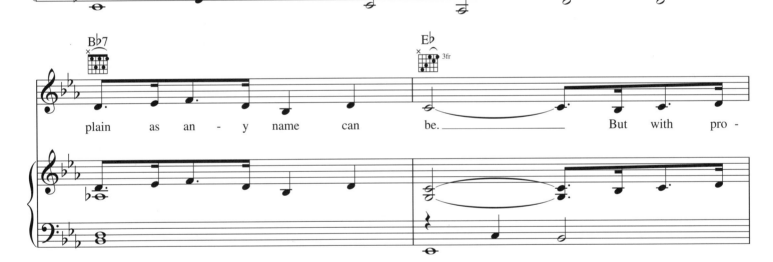

plain as an - y name can be. _____ But with pro -

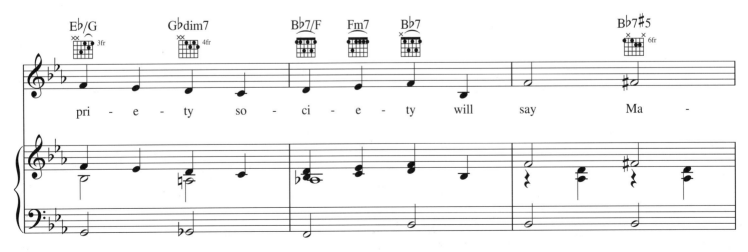

pri - e - ty so - ci - e - ty will say Ma -

rie. _____ But it was Mar - y, Mar - y,

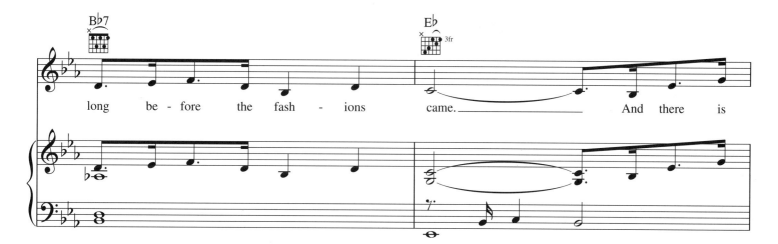

long be - fore the fash - ions came. _____ And there is

some - thing there that sounds so fair, it's a

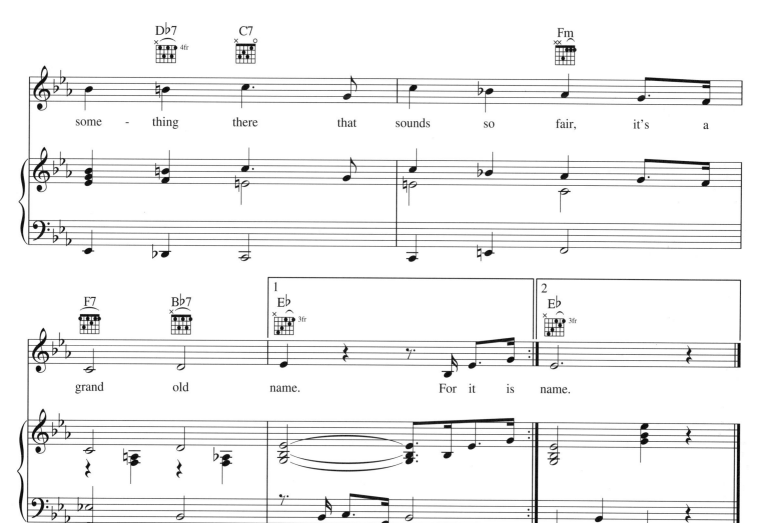

grand old name. For it is name.

McSORLEY TWINS

Traditional Irish Folksong

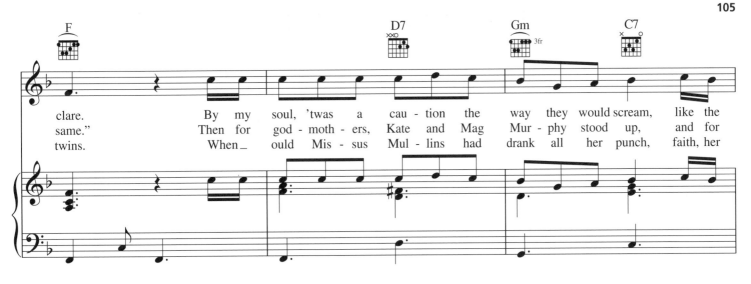

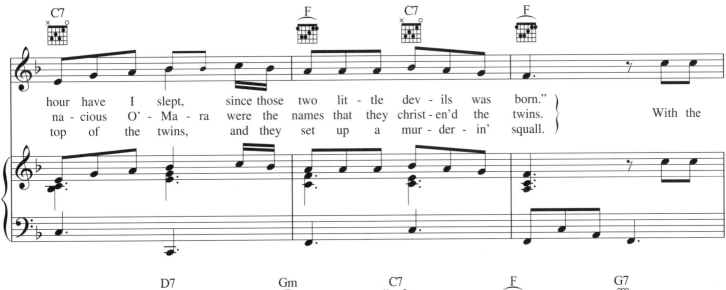

pins. Such an el-e-gant time at the christ-'nin' we had, of Mc-

Sor-ley's most beau-ti-ful twins.

Says
When the twins.
Then

Additional Lyrics

4. Then Mrs. McSorley jumped up in a rage,
And she threatened Miss Mullinses' life.
Says old Denny Mullins, "I'll beat the first man
That'd first lay a hand on my wife."
The McGanns and the Geohgans, they had an old grudge,
And Mag Murphy piched into the Flynns.
They fought like the devil, turned over the bed,
And they smothered the poor little twins.

MICK McGUIRE

Traditional Irish Folksong

Oh, me name is Mick Mc-Guire____ and I'll quick-ly tell to
first time that I met her was at the dance at Tar-ma-
now that we are mar-ried, sure, her moth-er's changed her

you of a young girl I ad-mired____ called____ Ka-ty Don-a-
gee, and I ver-y kind-ly asked her if she'd dance a step with
mind. Just be-cause I spent the leg-a-cy her fa-ther left be-

hue. She was fair and fat and for-ty, and be-lieve me when I
me. Then I asked if I could see her home, if I'd be go-in' her
hind. She____ has-n't got the de-cen-cy to bid me time of

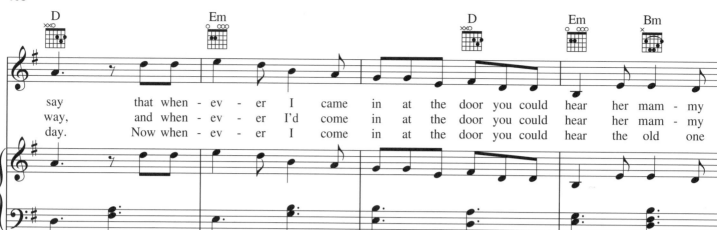

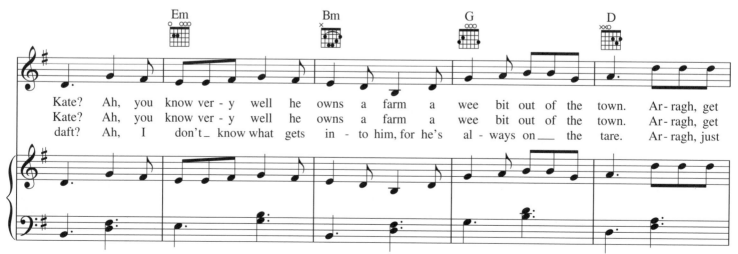

up out of that, you im-pu-dent brat, and let Mis-ter Mc-Guire sit down."
up out of that, you im-pu-dent brat, and let Mis-ter Mc-Guire sit down." Did-dle e dow-dle-ow-dle-
sit where you are and nev-er you dare to give old __ Mc-Guire the chair."

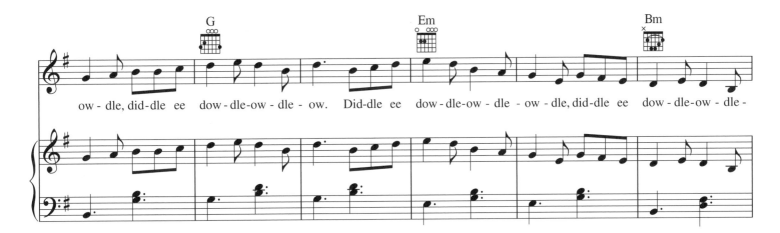

ow - dle, did-dle ee dow-dle-ow-dle-ow. Did-dle ee dow-dle-ow-dle-ow-dle, did-dle ee dow-dle-ow-dle-

"Ah, you know ver-y well he owns that farm a wee bit out of the town. Ar-ragh, get
"Ah, you know ver-y well he owns that farm a wee bit out of the town. Ar-ragh, get
"Ah, I don't __ know what gets in - to him for he's al - ways on __ the tare. Ar-ragh, just

1, 2
3

up out of that, you im-pu-dent brat, and let Mis-ter Mc-Guire sit down." Now, the
up out of that, you im-pu-dent brat, and let Mis-ter Mc-Guire sit down." Ah, but
sit where you are and nev-er you dare to give old __ Mc-Guire the   chair."

MINSTREL BOY

Traditional Irish Folksong

The min-strel boy __ to the war is gone. In the
min-strel fell __ but the foe-man's chain could not

ranks of death __ you'll find __ him. His fa-ther's sword __ he has
bring his proud __ soul un - der. The harp he loved __ nev-er

gird - ed on, and his wild harp slung __ be-hind __ him.
spoke a - gain, for he tore its cords __ a - sun - der and

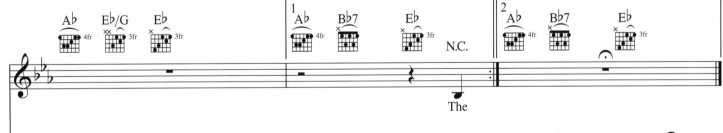

MRS. MURPHY'S CHOWDER

Traditional Irish Folksong

Moderately fast

Won't you

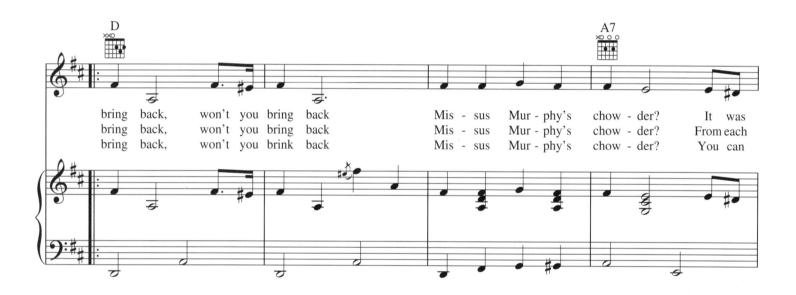

bring back, won't you bring back Mis - sus Mur - phy's chow - der? It was
bring back, won't you bring back Mis - sus Mur - phy's chow - der? From each
bring back, won't you brink back Mis - sus Mur - phy's chow - der? You can

tune - ful, ev - 'ry spoon - ful made you yo - del loud - er.
help - ing, you'll be yelp - ing for a head - ache pow - der. And
pack it, you can stack it all a - round the lard - er. The

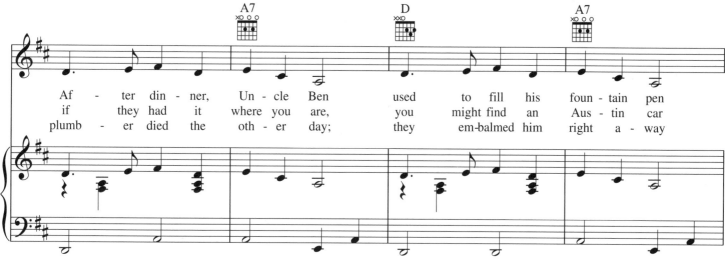

Af - ter din - ner, Un - cle Ben / used to fill his foun - tain pen
if they had it where you are, / used you might find an Aus - tin car
plumb - er died the oth - er day; / they em-balmed him right a - way

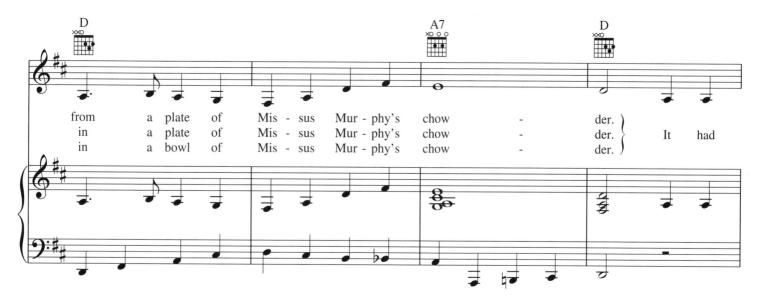

from a plate of Mis - sus Mur - phy's chow - der.
in a plate of Mis - sus Mur - phy's chow - der. } It had
in a bowl of Mis - sus Mur - phy's chow - der.

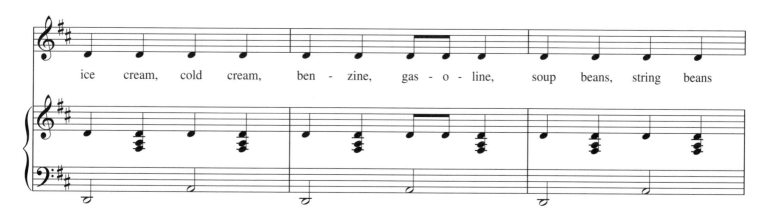

ice cream, cold cream, ben - zine, gas - o - line, soup beans, string beans

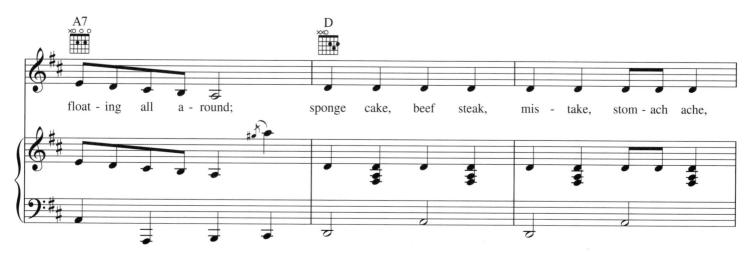

float - ing all a - round; sponge cake, beef steak, mis - take, stom - ach ache,

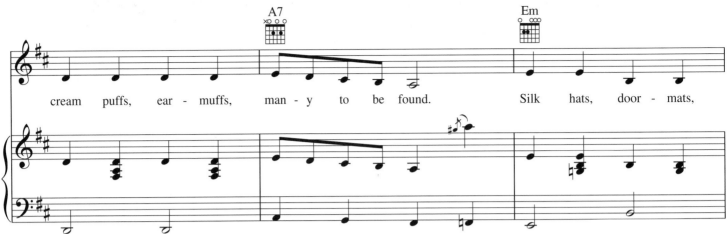

cream puffs, ear-muffs, man-y to be found. Silk hats, door-mats,

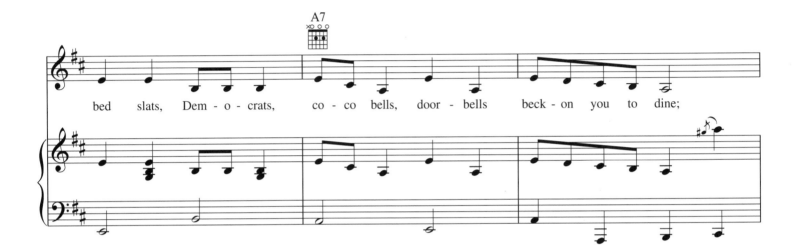

bed slats, Dem-o-crats, co-co bells, door-bells beck-on you to dine;

meat-balls, fish balls, moth balls, can-non balls, come on in, the

chow-der's fine! Won't you chow-der's fine!

8vb

THE MOUNTAINS OF MOURNE

Traditional Irish Folk Melody
Words by PERCY FRENCH

D

wheat, but there's gangs of them dig - ging for
ball, they ___ don't wear no top to for their
cream, but ___ let me re - mark with re -

G ... **C**

gold in the street. At least when I
dress - es at all. Oh, I've seen them me -
gard to the same, that if that those

G

asked them, that's what I was told, so I
self, and you could not in truth say that
ros - es you ven - ture to sip, the ___

A7

just took a hand at this dig - ging for
if they were bound all for come a ball or a
col - ors might all come a - way on your

MOLLY BAWN

Words and Music by
SAMUEL LOVER

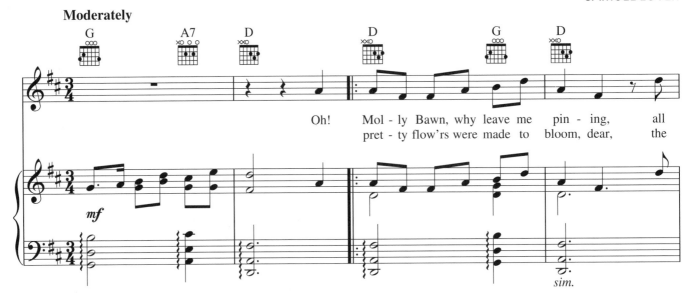

Oh! Mol - ly Bawn, why leave me pin - ing, all
pret - ty flow'rs were made to bloom, dear, the

lone - ly wait - ing here for you? While the stars a - bove are bright - ly shin - ing, be -
pret - ty stars were made to shine, and the pret - ty girls were made for boys, dear, and

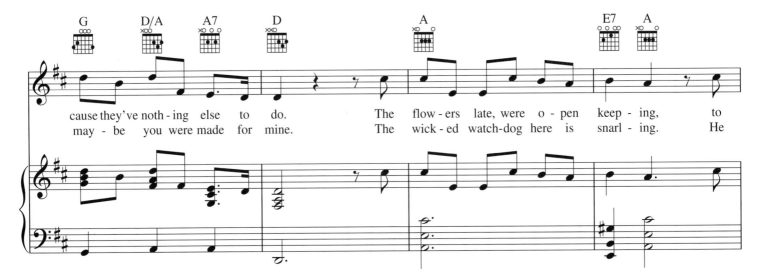

cause they've noth - ing else to do. The flow - ers late, were o - pen keep - ing, to
may - be you were made for mine. The wick - ed watch-dog here is snarl - ing. He

MOLLY MALONE
(Cockles & Mussels)

Traditional Irish Melody

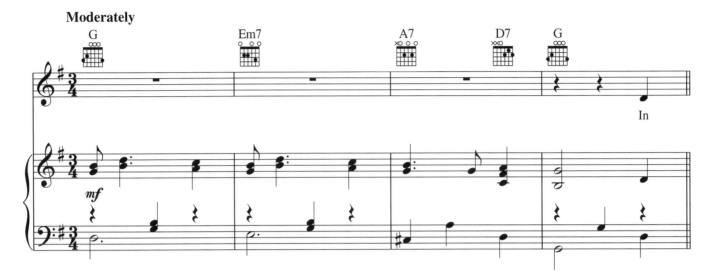

In

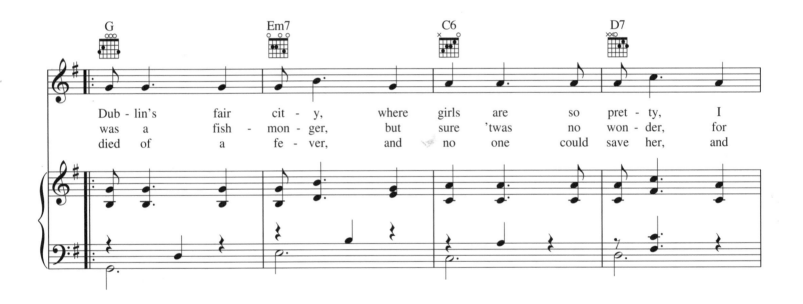

Dub - lin's fair cit - y, where girls are so pret - ty, I
was a fish - mon - ger, but sure 'twas no won - der, for
died of a fe - ver, and no one could save her, and

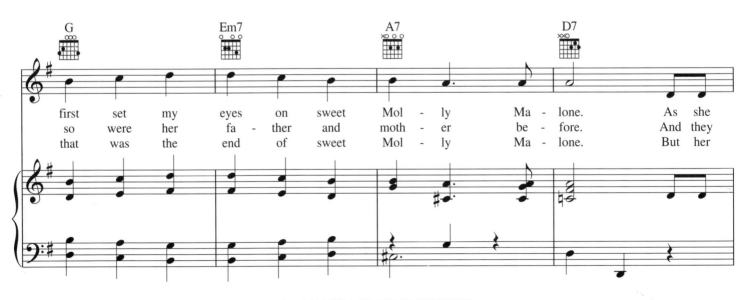

first set my eyes on sweet Mol - ly Ma - lone. As she
so were her fa - ther and moth - er be - fore. And they
that was the end of sweet Mol - ly Ma - lone. But her

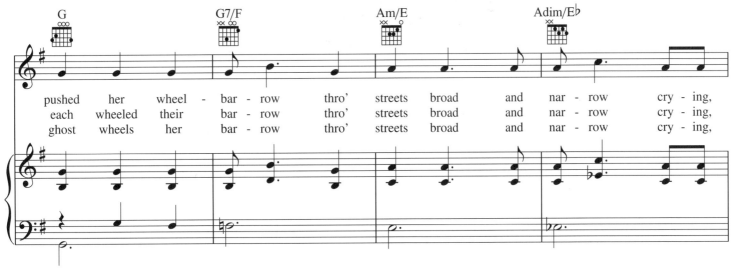

pushed her wheel - bar - row thro' streets broad and nar - row cry - ing,
each wheeled their bar - row thro' streets broad and nar - row cry - ing,
ghost wheels her bar - row thro' streets broad and nar - row cry - ing,

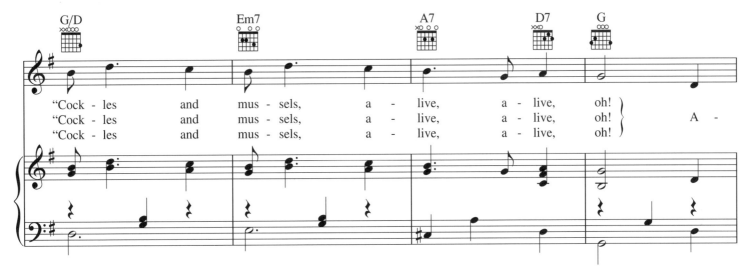

"Cock - les and mus - sels, a - live, a - live, oh!
"Cock - les and mus - sels, a - live, a - live, oh!
"Cock - les and mus - sels, a - live, a - live, oh!   A -

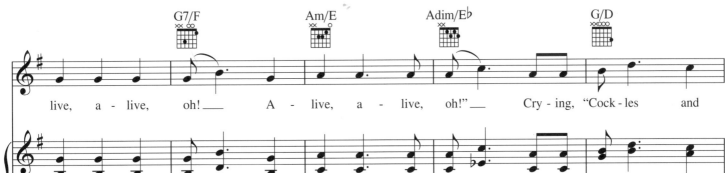

live, a - live, oh! ___ A - live, a - live, oh!" ___ Cry - ing, "Cock - les and

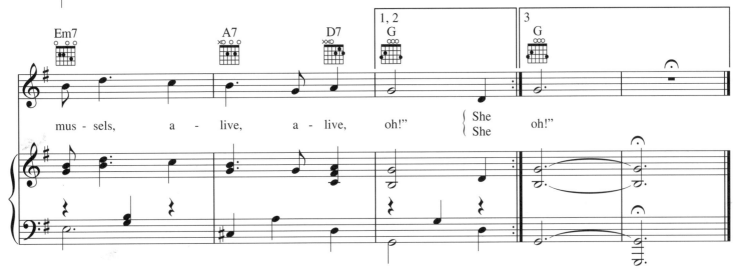

mus - sels, a - live, a - live, oh!"   She   oh!"
She

MOTHER MACHREE

Words by RIDA JOHNSON YOUNG
Music by CHAUNCEY OLCOTT
and ERNEST R. BALL

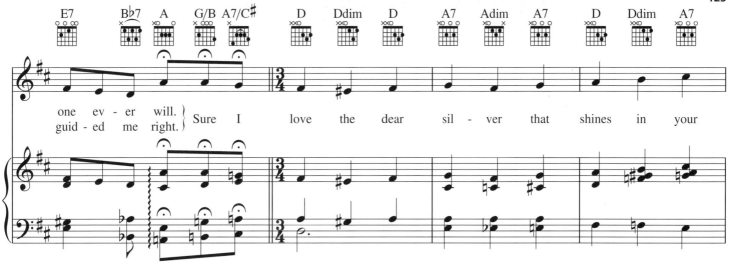

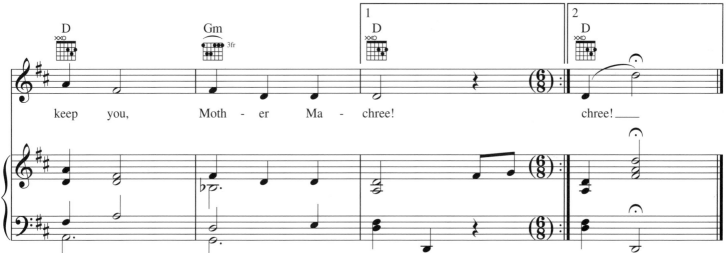

MY WILD IRISH ROSE

Words and Music by
CHAUNCEY OLCOTT

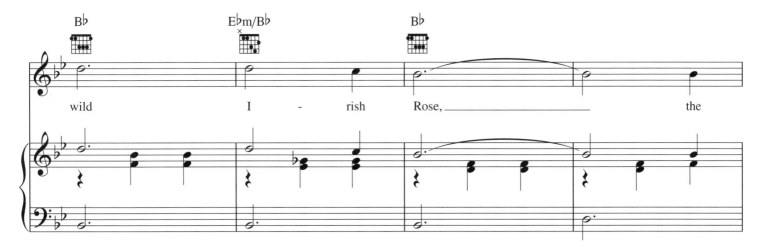

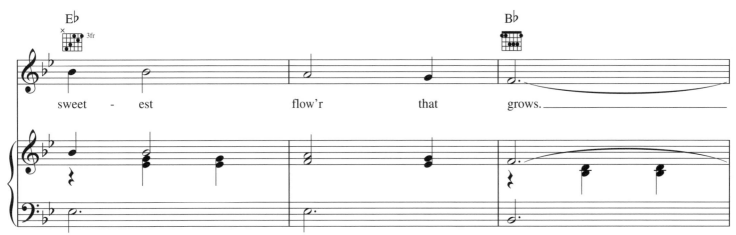

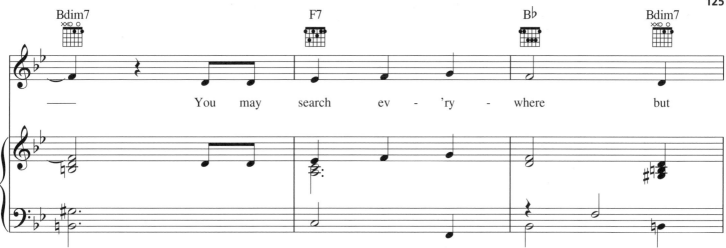

You may search ev - 'ry - where but

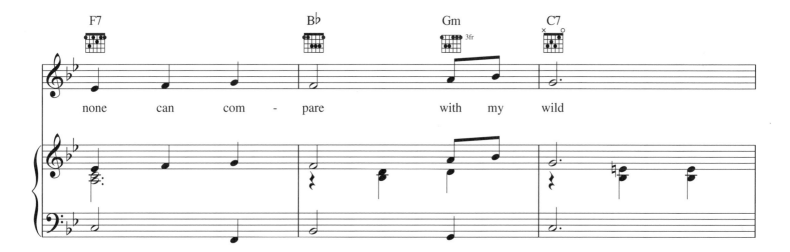

none can com - pare with my wild

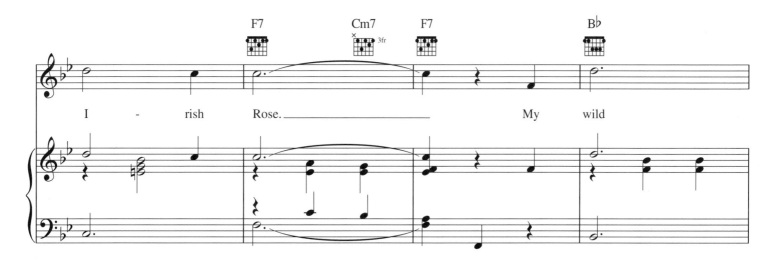

I - rish Rose._____ My wild

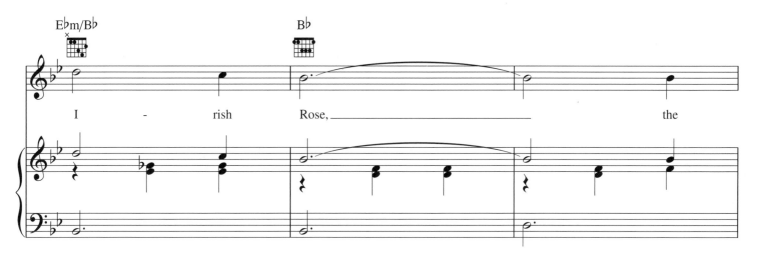

I - rish Rose,_____ the

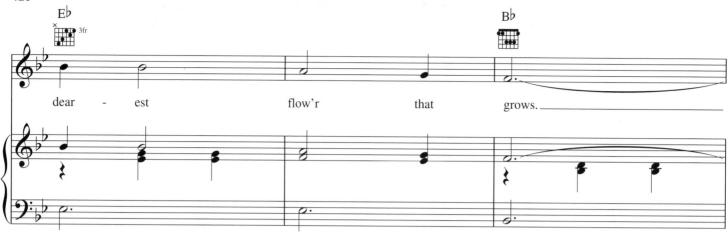

dear - est flow'r that grows.

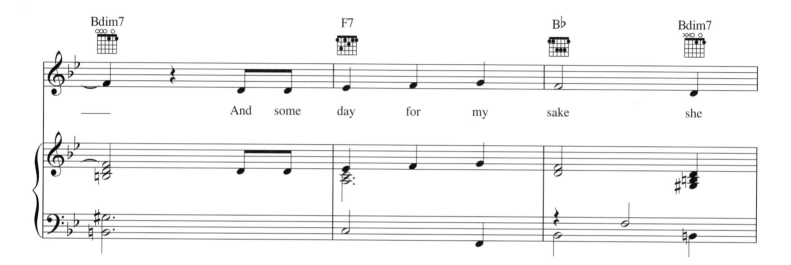

And some day for my sake she

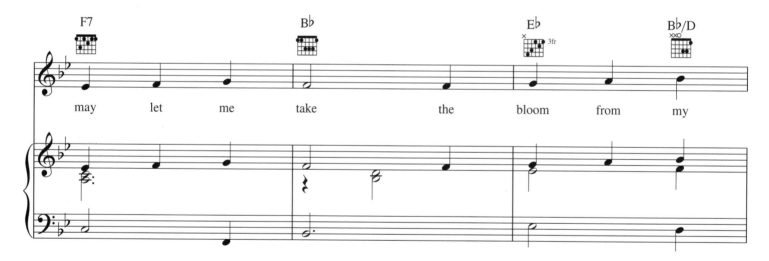

may let me take the bloom from my

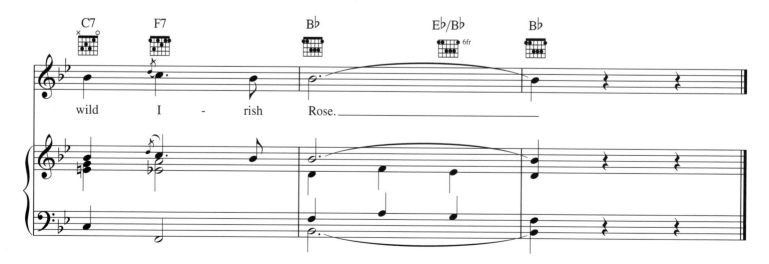

wild I - rish Rose.

A NATION ONCE AGAIN

Words and Music by
THOMAS DAVIS

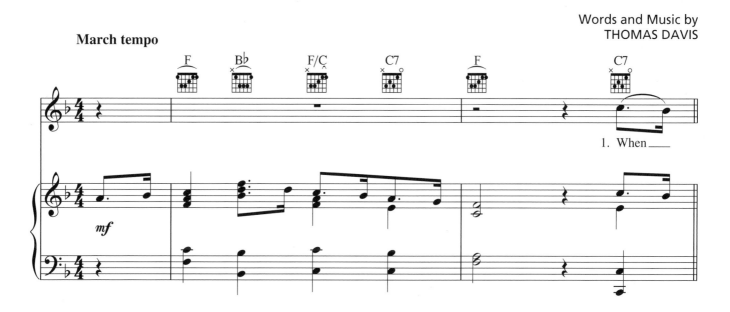

1. When __

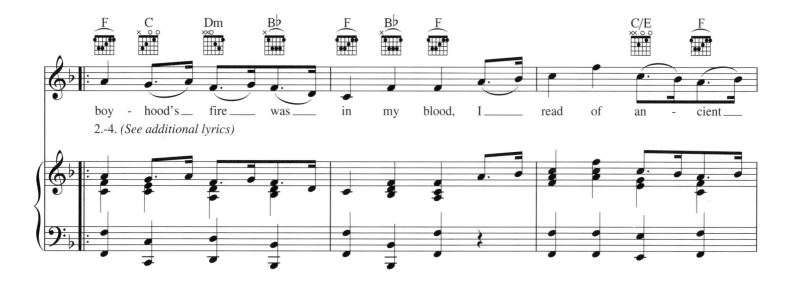

boy - hood's __ fire __ was __ in my blood, I __ read of an - cient __

2.-4. *(See additional lyrics)*

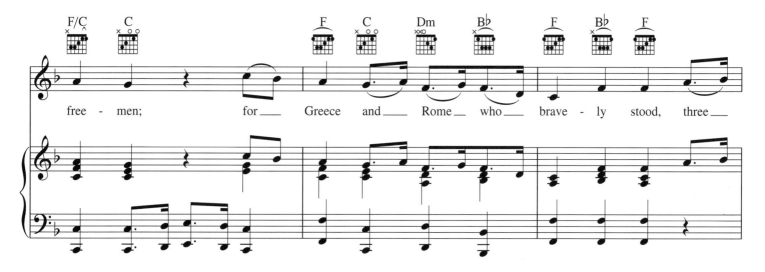

free - men; for __ Greece and __ Rome __ who __ brave - ly stood, three __

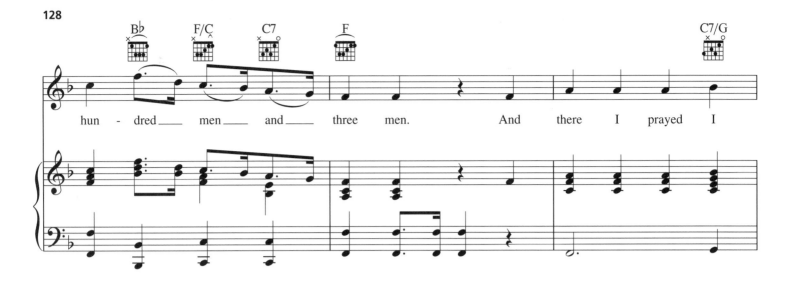

hun - dred___ men___ and___ three men.   And   there   I   prayed   I

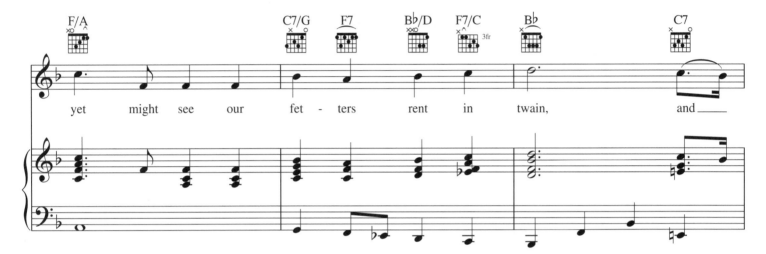

yet   might   see   our   fet - ters   rent   in   twain,   and___

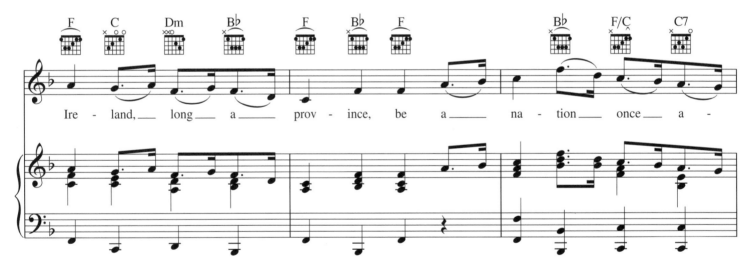

Ire - land,___ long___ a___ prov - ince,   be   a___ na - tion___ once   a -

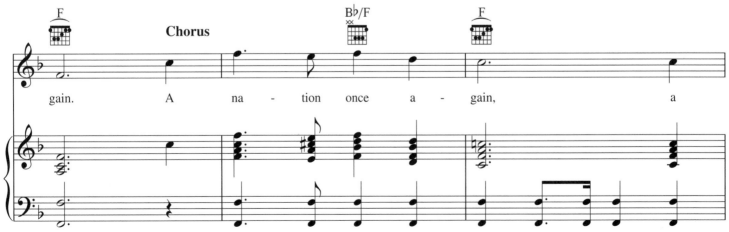

gain.   A   na - tion   once   a - gain,   a

Additional Lyrics

2. And from that time, through wildest woe,
   That hope has shown a far light;
   Nor could love's brightest summer glow
   Outshine that solemn starlight.
   It seemed to watch above my head
   In forum, field and fane;
   Its angel voice sang 'round my bed,
   "A nation once again."
   Chorus

3. It whispered too, that "Freedom's Ark"
   And service high and holy,
   Would be profaned by feelings dark
   And passions vain or lowly;
   For freedom comes from God's right hand,
   And needs a Godly train,
   And righteous men must make our land
   A nation once again.
   Chorus

4. So as I grew from boy to man,
   I bent me at that bidding;
   My spirit of each selfish plan
   And cruel passion ridding.
   For thus I hoped some day to aid.
   Oh! Can such hope be vain
   When my dear country shall be made
   A nation once again?
   Chorus

O'DONNELL ABOO

Words and Music by
M.J. McCANN

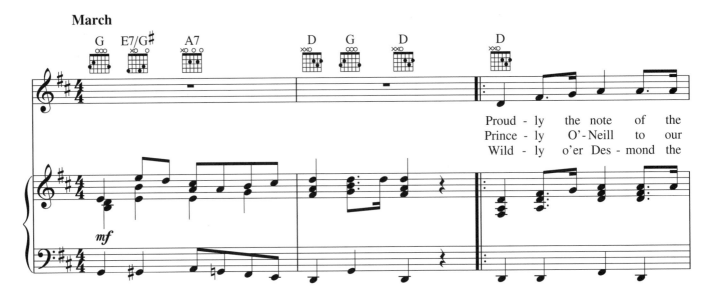

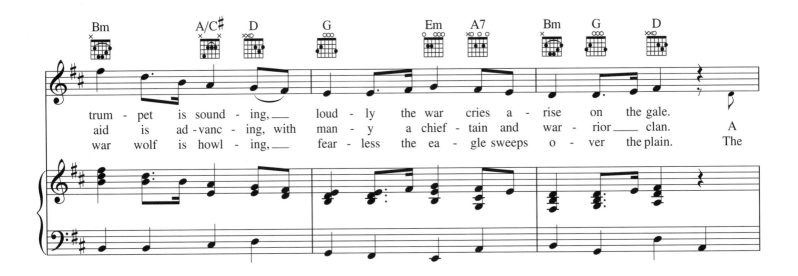

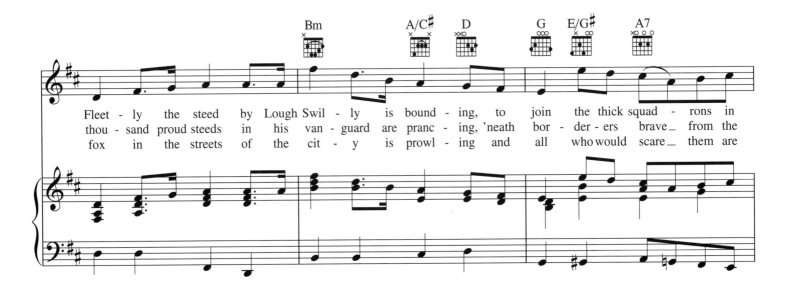

OFT IN THE STILLY NIGHT

Traditional Irish Folksong

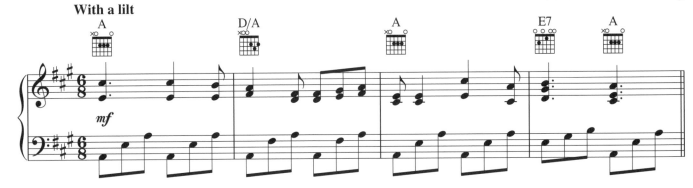

With a lilt

Oft in the stil-ly night, ere slum-ber's chain has bound ___ me,
When I re-mem-ber all the friends, so linked to-geth - er,

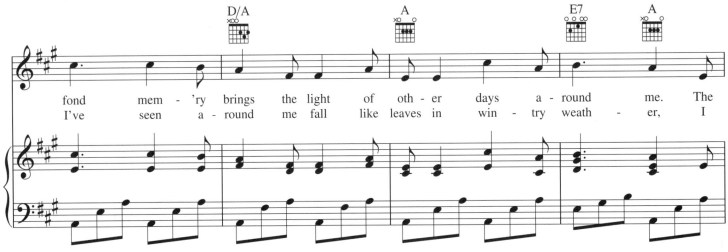

fond mem-'ry brings the light of oth-er days a-round me. The
I've seen a-round me fall like leaves in win-try weath-er, I

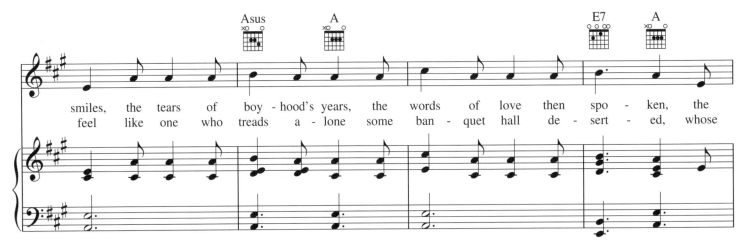

smiles, the tears of boy-hood's years, the words of love then spo-ken, the
feel like one who treads a-lone some ban-quet hall de-sert - ed, whose

eyes that shone, now dimmed and gone, the cheer - ful hearts now bro - ken.
lights are fled, whose gar - land's dead, and all but he de - part - ed.

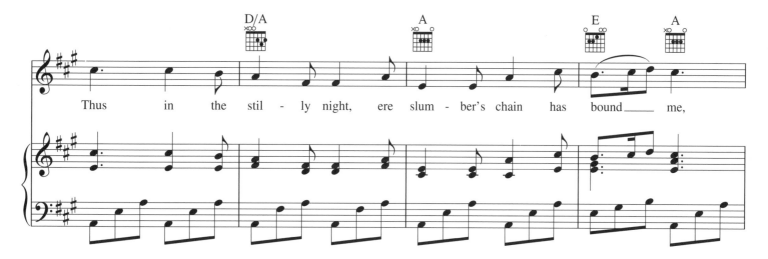

Thus in the stil - ly night, ere slum - ber's chain has bound____ me,

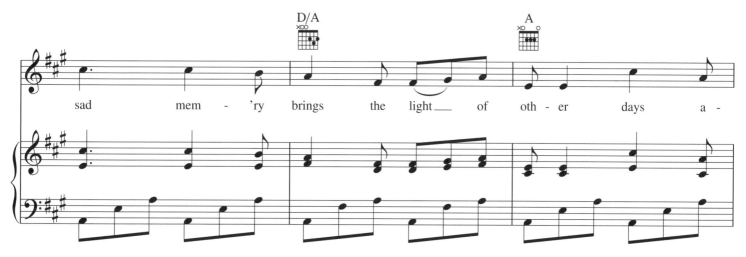

sad mem - 'ry brings the light____ of oth - er days a -

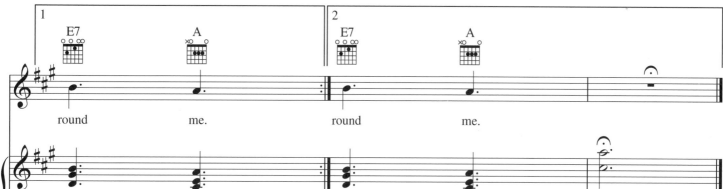

round me. round me.

PEG O' MY HEART

Words by ALFRED BRYAN
Music by FRED FISHER

Moderately

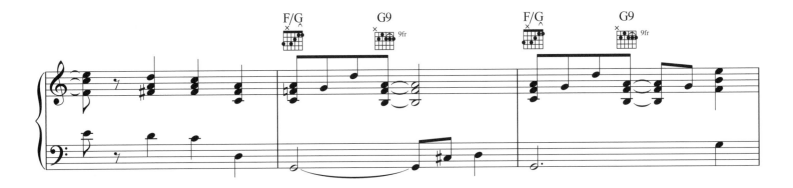

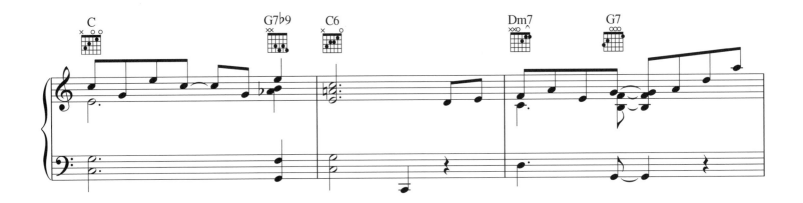

Oh! my heart's in a whirl, __ o-ver one lit-tle girl, __ I

When your heart's full of fears, __ and your eyes full of tears, __ I'll

love her, I love___ her, yes, I do,_____ al-tho' her heart is far a-
kiss them, I'll kiss___ them all a-way;_____ for, like the gold that's in your

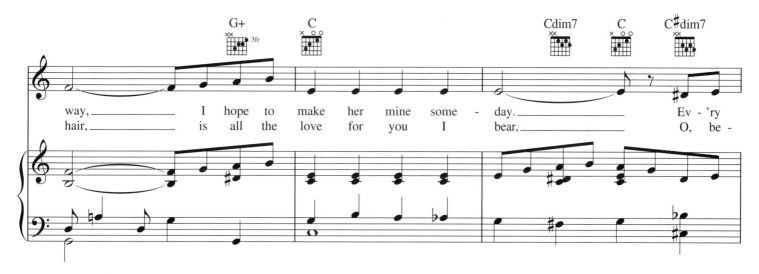

way,_____ I hope to make her mine some-day._____ Ev-'ry
hair,_____ is all the love for you I bear,_____ O, be-

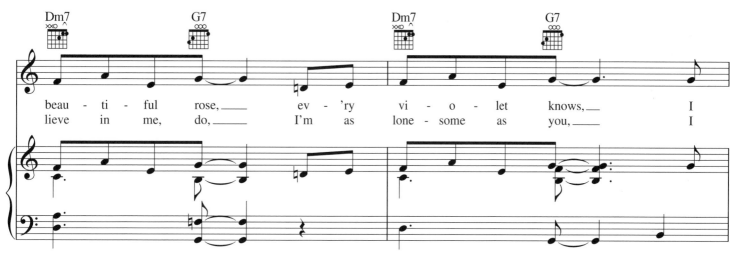

beau-ti-ful rose,___ ev-'ry vi-o-let knows,___ I
lieve in me, do,___ I'm as lone-some as you,___ I

love her, I love___ her fond and true,_____ and her
miss you, I miss___ her you all the day,_____ let the

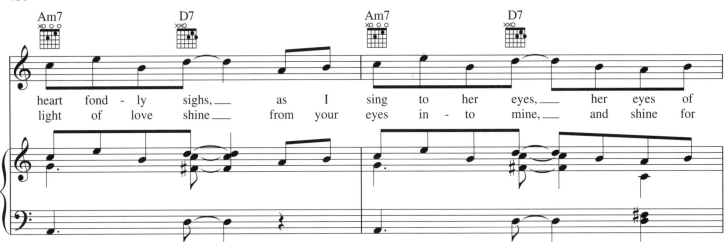

heart fond - ly sighs, ___ as I sing to her eyes, ___ her eyes of
light of love shine ___ from your eyes in - to mine, ___ and shine for

blue, ___ sweet eyes of blue, my dar - ling! ⎬ Peg o' my heart, ___
aye, ___ sweet - heart for aye, my dar - ling! ⎬

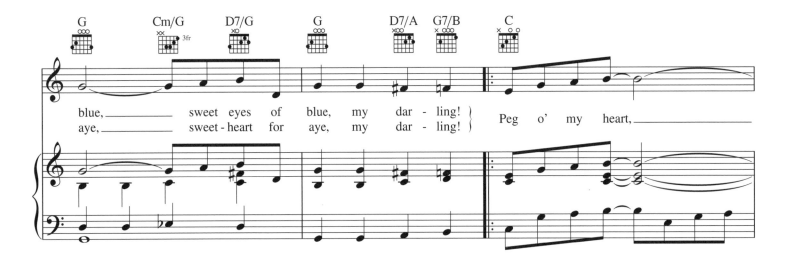

___ I love you, we'll nev - er part, ___ I love you,

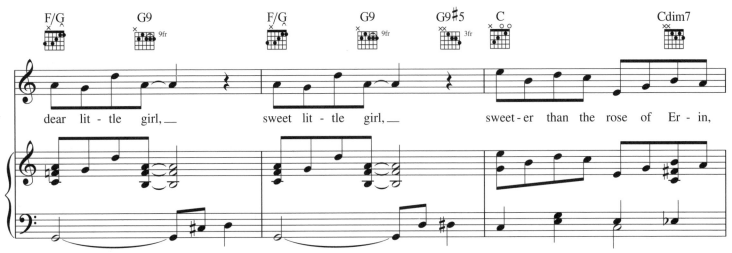

dear lit - tle girl, ___ sweet lit - tle girl, ___ sweet - er than the rose of Er - in,

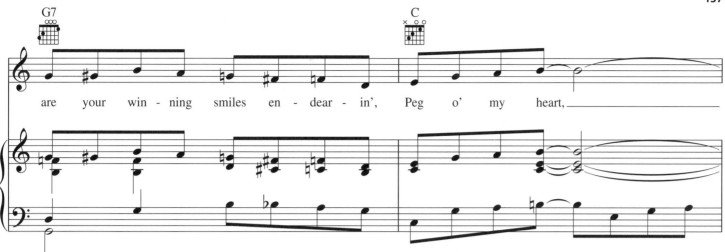

are your win-ning smiles en-dear-in', Peg o' my heart, ____

____ your glanc-es with I-rish art ____ en-trance us,

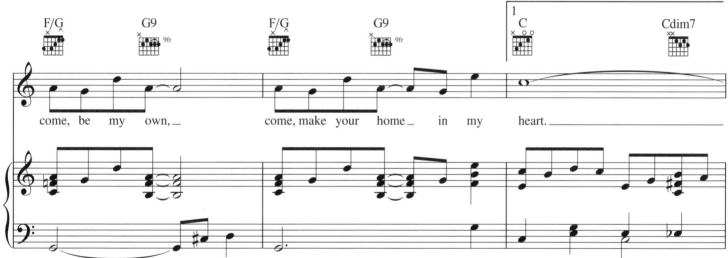

come, be my own, ____ come, make your home ___ in my heart. ____

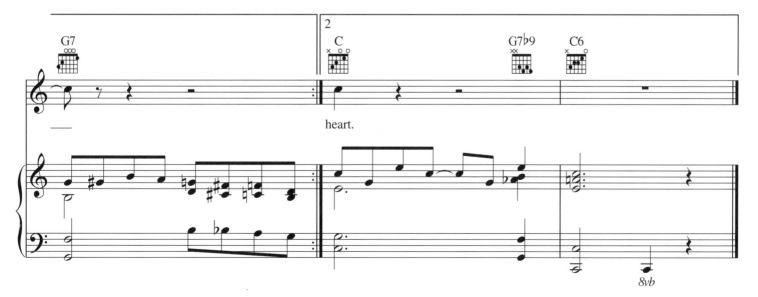

heart.

8vb

PEGGY O'NEIL

Words and Music by HARRY PEASE,
ED. G. NELSON and GILBERT DODGE

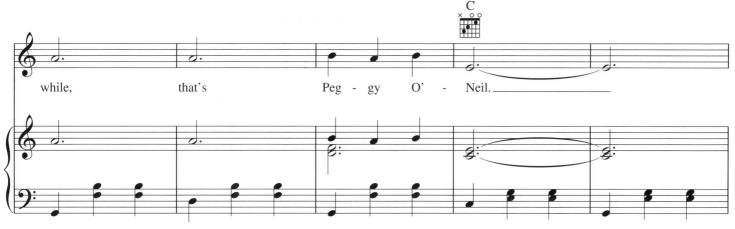

while, that's Peg - gy O' - Neil. _____

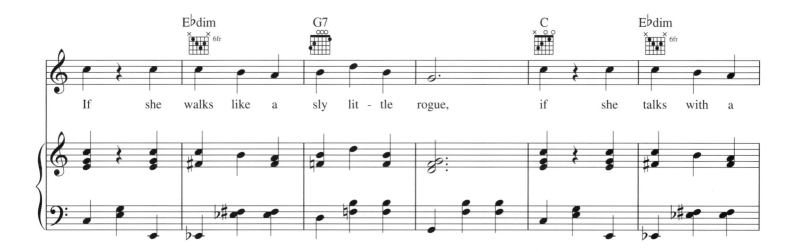

If she walks like a sly lit - tle rogue, if she talks with a

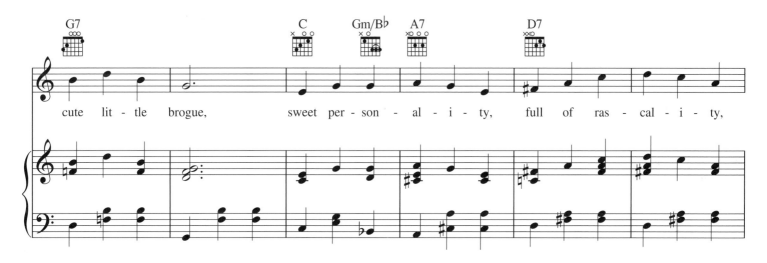

cute lit - tle brogue, sweet per - son - al - i - ty, full of ras - cal - i - ty,

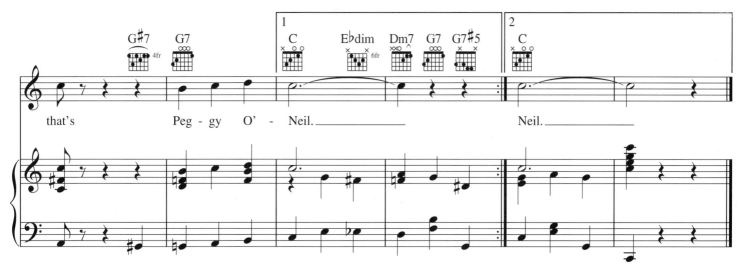

that's Peg - gy O' - Neil. _____ Neil. _____

PRETTY GIRL MILKING A COW

Traditional Irish Folksong

Plaintively

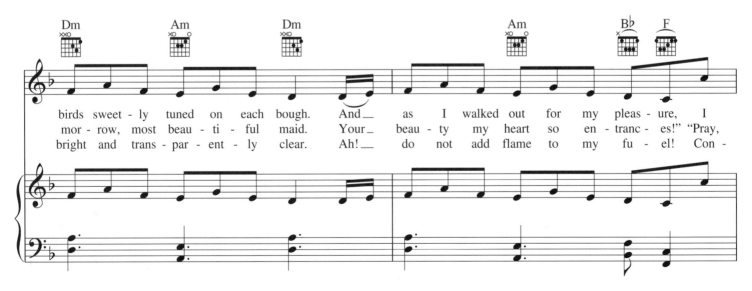

saw — a — maid milk-ing her cow. Her — voice — so en-chant-ing, me-lo-dious, left —
sir, — do — not — ban-ter," she — said. "I'm — not — such a rare pre-cious jew-el, that —
sent — but — to — love me, my — dear." Ah! — had — I the lamp of A-lad-din, or the

me quite — un-a-ble to — go. My — heart it was load-ed with sor-row for —
I should — en-am-our you so. I — am but a poor lit-tle milk-girl," says —
wealth of — the — Af-ri-can — shore, I'd rath-er be poor in a cot-tage with —

*Col-leen dhas — cru-then na - moe. Then — Col-leen dhas — cru-then na - moe.
Col-leen dhas — cru-then na - moe. "The —

* The pretty girl milking her cow.

THE QUEEN OF CONNEMARA

Traditional Irish Folksong

Oh, __ my boat can safe-ly float in __ the teeth of wind and
load - ed down with fish till __ the wa - ter lips the
light shines out a - far, and __ it keeps me from dis -

weath - er, and out - race the fast - est hook - er be - tween Gal - way and Kin -
gun - wale, not a drop she'll take on board her that __ would wash a fly a -
may - ing when the skies are ink a - bove us, and __ the sea runs white with

sale. When the black floor of the o - cean and the white foam rush to
way. From the fleet she'll slip out swift - ly like a grey - hound from her
foam. In a cot in Con - ne - ma - ra there's a wife and wee one

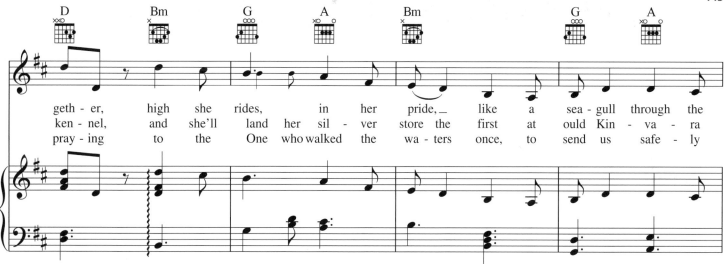

geth - er, high she rides, in her pride,__ like a sea - gull through the
ken - nel, and she'll land her sil - ver store the first at ould Kin - va - ra
pray - ing to the One who walked the wa - ters once, to send us safe - ly

gale.
quay. Oh, she's neat! Oh,__ she's sweet!____ She's a beau - ty ev - 'ry
home.

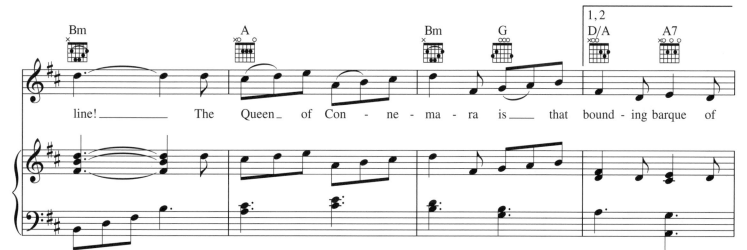

line!_____ The Queen__ of Con - ne - ma - ra is__ that bound - ing barque of

1, 2

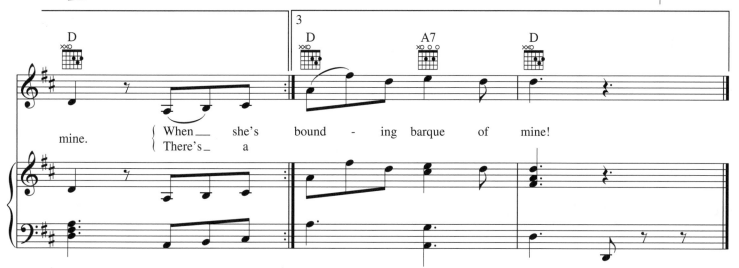

mine.

3

When__ she's bound - ing barque of mine!
There's__ a

THE ROSE OF TRALEE

Words by C. MORDAUNT SPENCER
Music by CHARLES W. GLOVER

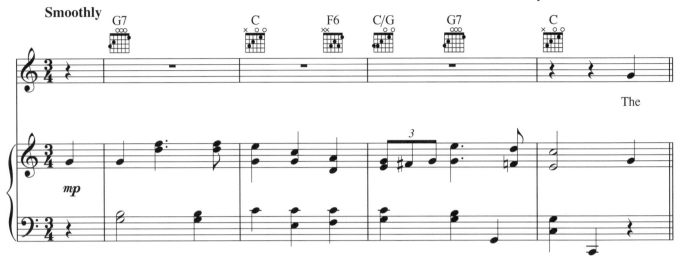

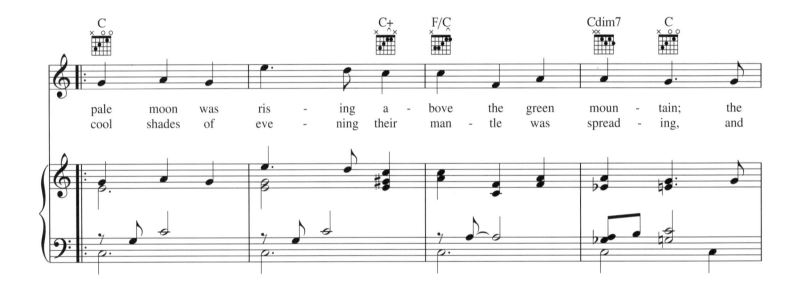

pale moon was ris - ing a - bove the green moun - tain; the
cool shades of eve - ning their man - tle was spread - ing, and

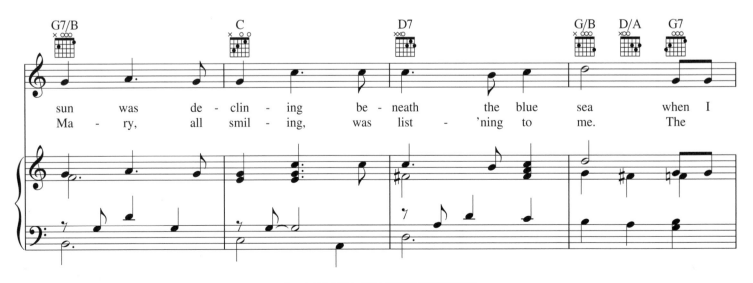

sun was de - clin - ing be - neath the blue sea; when I
Ma - ry, all smil - ing, was list - 'ning to me. The

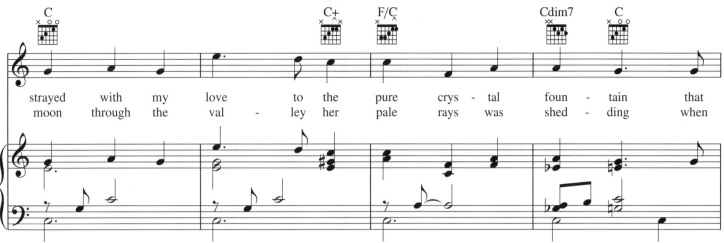

strayed with my love to the pure crys - tal foun - tain that
moon through the val - ley her pure pale rays was shed - ding that when

stands in the beau - ti - ful vale of Tra -
I won the heart of the rose of Tra -

lee. She was } love - ly and fair as the
lee. Though_ }

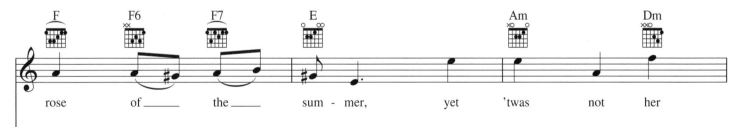

rose of _____ the _____ sum - mer, yet 'twas not her

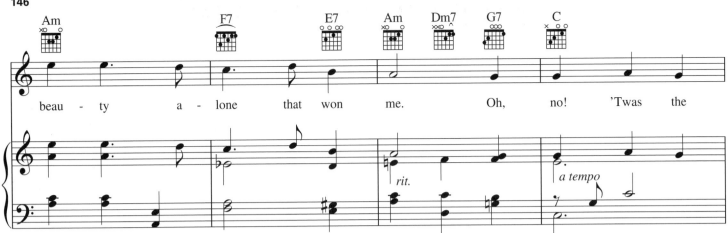

beauty a - lone that won me. Oh, no! 'Twas the

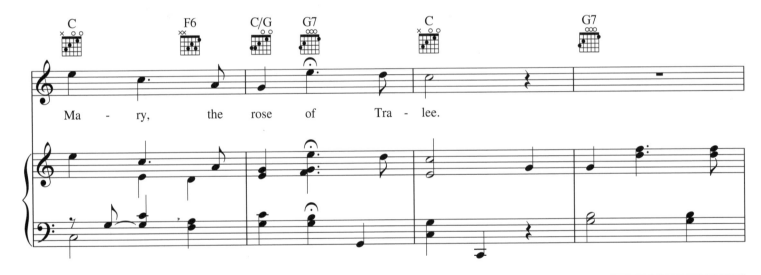

truth in her eye ev - er dawn - ing that made me love

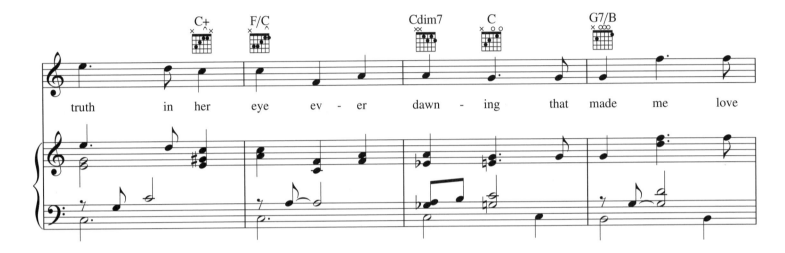

Ma - ry, the rose of Tra - lee.

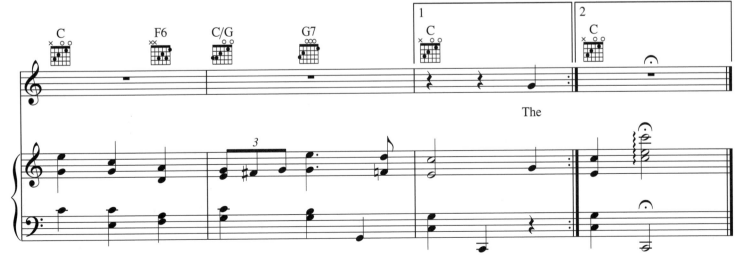

The

SAILOR'S HORNPIPE

Traditional Irish Sea Chantey

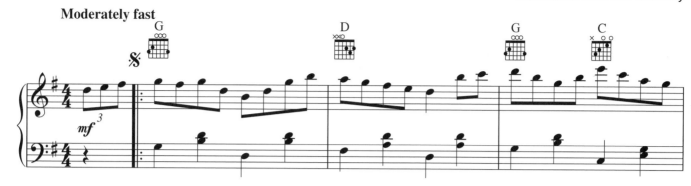

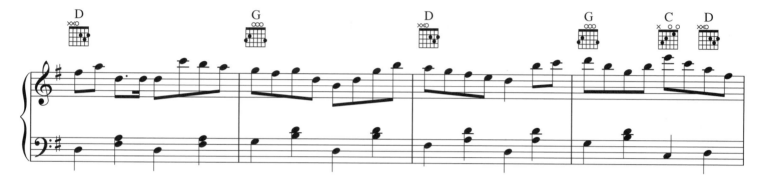

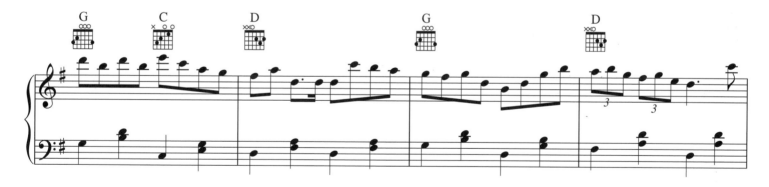

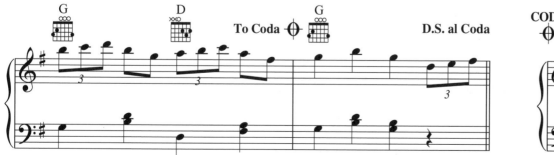

SEVEN DRUNKEN NIGHTS

Traditional Irish Folksong

1. Well, as I came home on Mon-day night, as drunk as drunk could be, I
2.-5. *(See additional lyrics)*

saw'r a horse out-side the door where my old horse should be. So, I called the wife and I said to her, "Will ya

kind-ly tell to me who owns that horse out-side the door where my old horse should be?"

Chorus

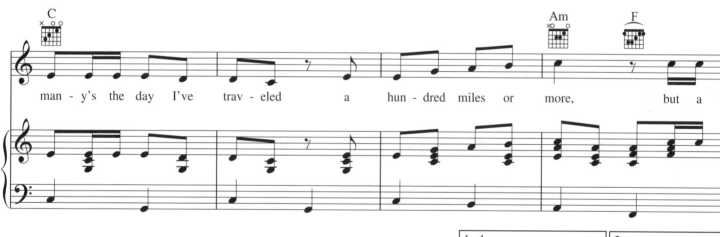

2. Now, as I came home on Tuesday night,
   As drunk as drunk could be,
   I saw'r a coat behind the door
   Where my old coat should be.
   So I called the wife and I said to her,
   "Will ya kindly tell to me,
   Who owns that coat behind the door
   Where my old coat should be?"

Chorus 2. Ah, you're drunk, you're drunk you silly old fool, till you cannot see.
   That's a lovely blanket that me mother sent to me.
   Well, many's the day I traveled a hundred miles or more,
   But buttons on a blanket sure I never seen before.

3. And as I went home on Wednesday night,
   As drunk as drunk could be,
   I saw'r a pipe upon the chair
   Where my old pipe should be.
   I calls the wife and I says to her,
   "Will ya kindly tell to me,
   Who owns that pipe upon the chair
   Where my old pipe should be?"

Chorus 3. Ah, you're drunk, you're drunk you silly old fool, still you cannot see.
   And that's a lovely tin whistle that me mother sent to me.
   Well, and many's the day I've traveled a hundred miles or more,
   But tobacco in a tin whistle sure I never seen before.

4. And as I went home on Thursday night,
   As drunk as drunk could be,
   I saw'r two boots beneath the bed
   Where my two boots should be.
   I called the wife and I said to her,
   "Will ya kindly tell to me,
   Who owns those boots beneath the bed
   Where my old boots should be?"

Chorus 4. Ah, you're drunk, you're drunk you silly old fool, until you cannot see.
   And that's me lovely geranium pots me mother sent to me.
   Well, it's many's the day I've traveled a hundred miles or more,
   But laces on a geranium pot I never seen before.

5. And as I went home on Friday night,
   As drunk as drunk could be,
   I saw'r a head upon the bed
   Where my old head should be.
   So, I called the wife and I said to her,
   "Will ya kindly tell to me,
   Who owns that head upon the bed
   Where my old head should be?"

Chorus 5. Ah, you're drunk, you're drunk you silly old fool, and still you cannot see.
   That's a baby boy that me mother sent to me.
   Hey, it's many's the day I've traveled a hundred miles or more,
   But a baby boy with whiskers on I never seen before.

THE SPINNING WHEEL SONG

Moderately slow

Words and Music by
J.F. WALLER

1. Mel - low the moon - light to shine is be - gin - ning.
2. What's the noise that I hear at the win - dow I won - der.
3. There's a form of the case - ment, the form of her true love.
4. *(See additional lyrics)*

Close by the win - dow young Ei - leen is spin - ning.
'Tis the lit - tle birds chirp - ing the hol - ly bush un - der.
And he whis - pers with face bent, "I'm wait - ing for you, love.

Bent o'er the fire her blind grand - moth - er sit - ting,
What makes you be shov - ing and mov - ing your stool on, an'
Set up from the stool, through the lat - tice step light - ly. We'll

Additional Lyrics

4. The maid shakes her head, on her lips lays her fingers,
    Steals up from the stool, longs to go and yet lingers.
    A frightened glance turns to her drowsy grandmother,
    Puts one foot on the stool, spins the wheel with the other.
    Slower and slower and slower the wheel swings,
    Lower and lower and lower the reel rings.
    Ere the reel and the wheel stop their ringing and moving,
    Through the grove the young lovers by the moonlight are roving.

THE SNOWY-BREASTED PEARL

Traditional Irish Folksong

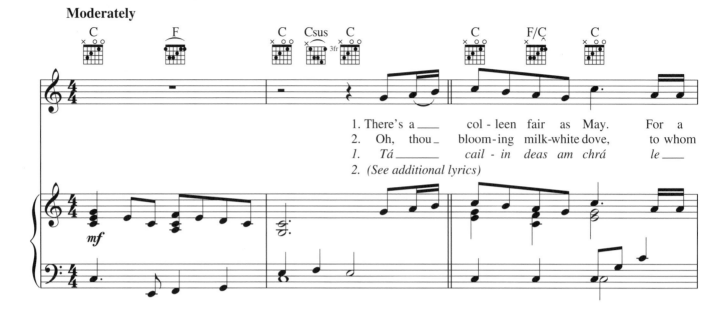

Additional Lyrics

2. *Is a chailín chailcee bhláith,*
   Dá dtugas searc is grá,
   Ná túir-se gach tráth dhom éara;
   'S a liacht ainnir mhín im dheáidh
   Le buaibh is maoin 'n-a láimh,
   Dá ngabhaimís it áit-se céile.
   Póg is míle fáilte
   Is barra geal do lámh'
   Sé 'n-iarrfainn-se go bráth mar spré leat;
   'S maran domh-sa taoi tú i ndán,
   A phéarla an bhrollaigh bháin,
   Nár thí mise slán ón aonach!

THE SPANISH LADY

Traditional Irish Folksong

As I went down to ___ Dub-lin cit - y, at the hour of
I went back through ___ Dub-lin cit - y, as the sun be -
wan-dered north and ___ I've wan-dered ___ south through Ston-y bat - ter and

twelve at night, who should I see but a Span-ish la - dy wash-ing her feet by
gan to set, who should I spy but the Span-ish la - dy catch-ing a moth in a
Pat - rick's close, up and a - round the ___ Glos - ter Dia - mond and back by Nap - per

can - dle - light. First she washed them, then she dried them o - ver a fire of
gold - en net. When she saw me, then she fled me, lift - ing her pet - ti - coat
Tan - dy's house. Old age has laid her hand on me, cold as a fire of

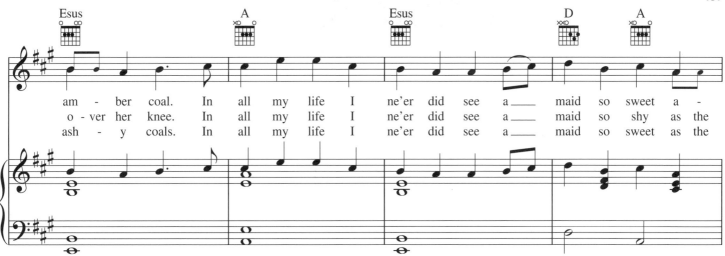

am - ber coal. In all my life I ne'er did see a___ maid so sweet a -
o - ver her knee. In all my life I ne'er did see a___ maid so shy as the
ash - y coals. In all my life I ne'er did see a___ maid so sweet as the

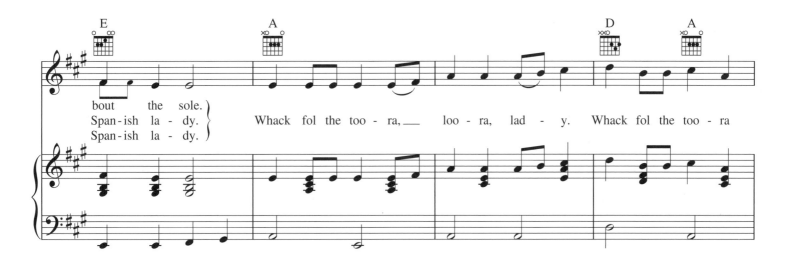

bout the sole. }
Span - ish la - dy. } Whack fol the too - ra,___ loo - ra, lad - y. Whack fol the too - ra
Span - ish la - dy. }

loo - ra - lay. Whack fol the too - ra,___ loo - ra, la - dy. Whack fol the too - ra

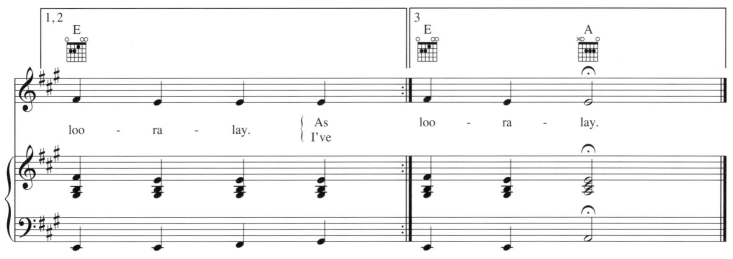

loo - ra - lay. { As   loo - ra - lay.
                 { I've

STAR OF COUNTY DOWN

Traditional Irish Folksong

Near to Ban - bridge town in the Coun - ty Down on a
on - ward sped, I___ scratched my head and I
har - vest fair she'll sure - ly be there, so I'll

morn - ing___ in Ju - ly, down a bo - reen green came a sweet cai - leen, and she
gazed with a feel - ing___ quare. There I said, said I to a pas - ser - by, "Who's the
dress in my Sun - day___ clothes. And I'll try sheep's eyes and de - lud - th'rin lies on the

smiled as she passed me by. Oh, she looked so neat from her two white feet to the
maid with the nut - brown hair?" Oh, he smiled at me, and with pride says he, "That's the
heart of the nut - brown Rose. No___ pipe I'll smoke, no___ horse I'll yoke, though my

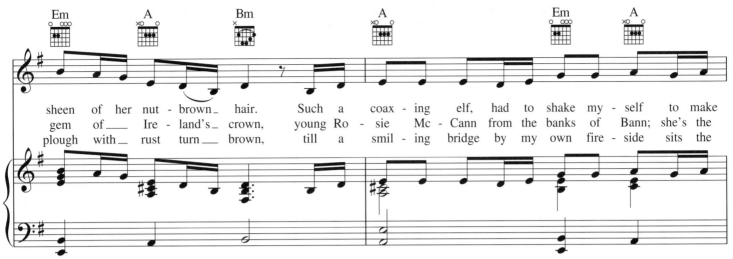

sheen of her nut - brown__ hair. Such a coax - ing elf, had to shake my - self to make
gem of ___ Ire - land's__ crown, young Ro - sie Mc - Cann from the banks of Bann; she's the
plough with__ rust turn__ brown, till a smil - ing bridge by my own fire - side sits the

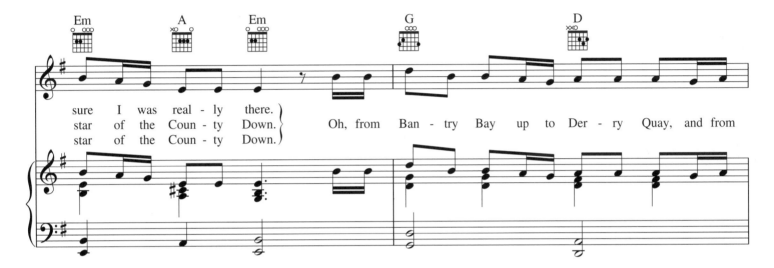

sure I was real - ly there.
star of the Coun - ty Down. Oh, from Ban - try Bay up to Der - ry Quay, and from
star of the Coun - ty Down.

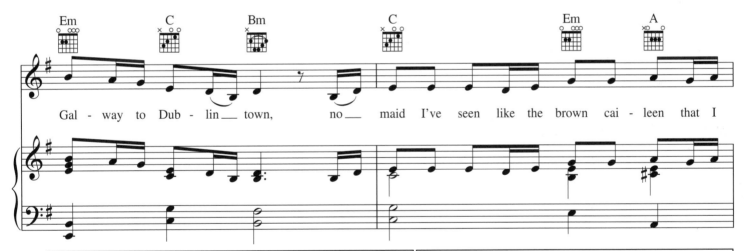

Gal - way to Dub - lin __ town, no __ maid I've seen like the brown cai - leen that I

1, 2
met in the Coun - ty Down.
As she   met in the Coun - ty Down.
At the

3

SWEET ROSIE O'GRADY

Words and Music by
MAUDE NUGENT

Moderately slow

don't mind tell - ing you that she's the sweet - est lit - tle Rose the

small en - gage - ment ring while in the trees the lit - tle birds this

Moderate Waltz

gar - den ev - er grew.

song they seemed to sing:

Sweet Ro - sie O' - Gra -

dy, my dear lit - tle Rose,

she's my stead - y la - dy, most

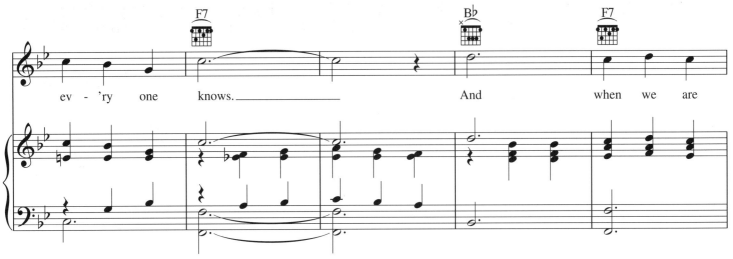

ev - 'ry one knows._____ And when we are

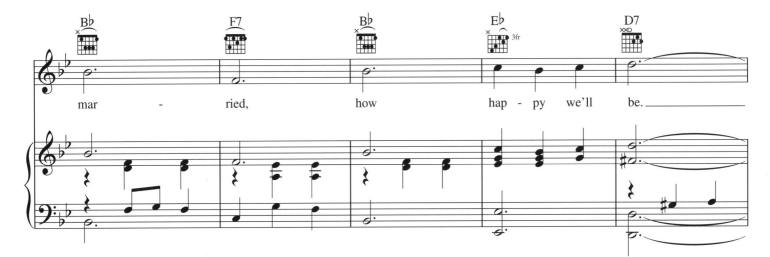

mar - ried, how hap-py we'll be._____

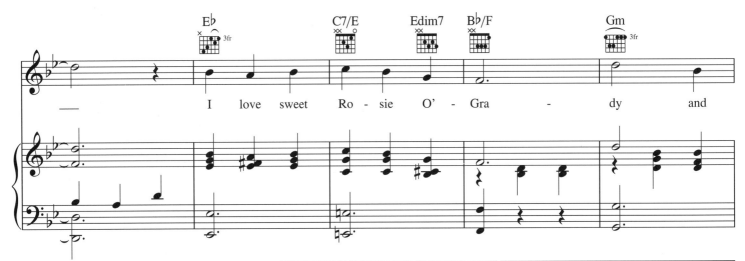

_____ I love sweet Ro - sie O' - Gra - dy and

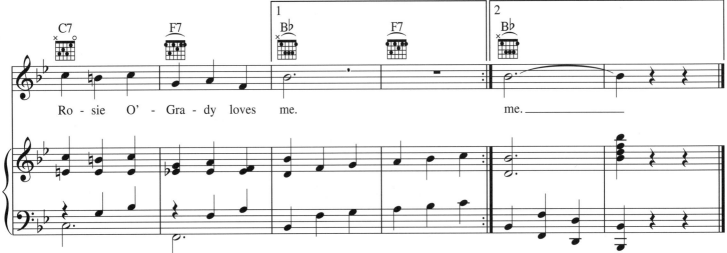

Ro - sie O' - Gra - dy loves me. me._____

WHERE THE RIVER SHANNON FLOWS

Words and Music by
JAMES J. RUSSELL

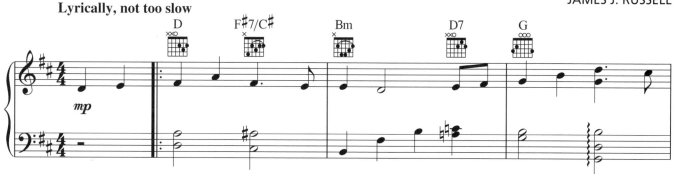

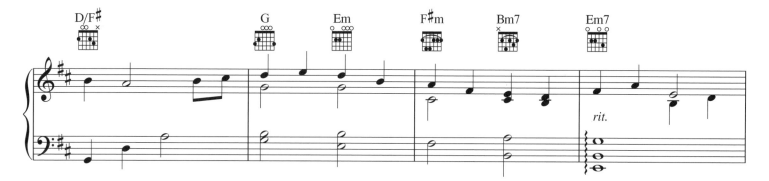

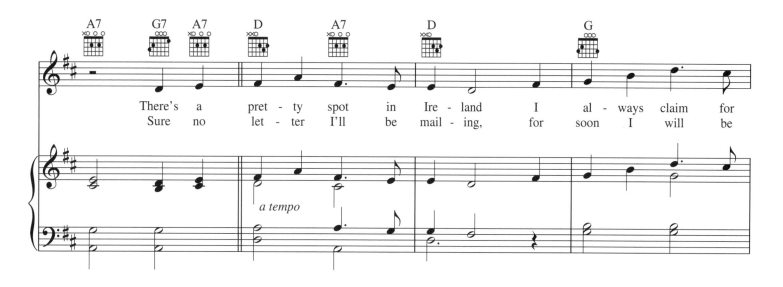

There's a pret-ty spot in Ire-land I al-ways claim for
Sure no let-ter I'll be mail-ing, for soon I will be

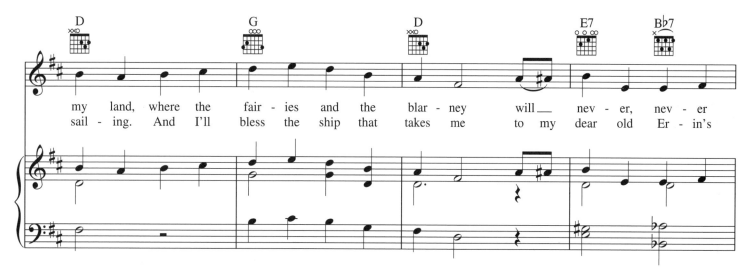

my land, where the fair-ies and the blar-ney will __ nev-er, nev-er
sail-ing. And I'll bless the ship that takes me to my dear old Er-in's

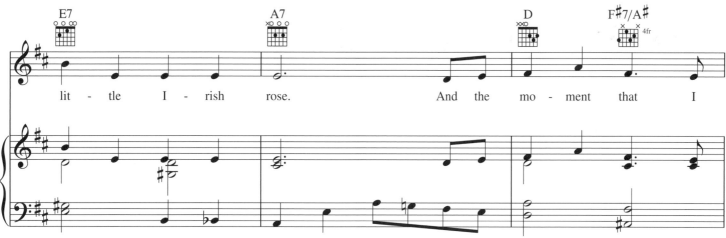

lit - tle I - rish rose.   And the mo - ment that   I

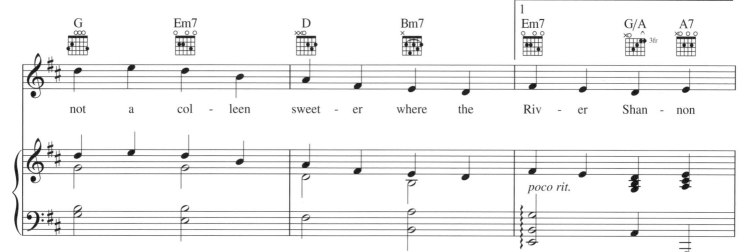

meet her,   with a   hug and kiss I'll   greet her,   for there's

not   a   col - leen sweet - er where   the Riv - er Shan - non

poco rit.

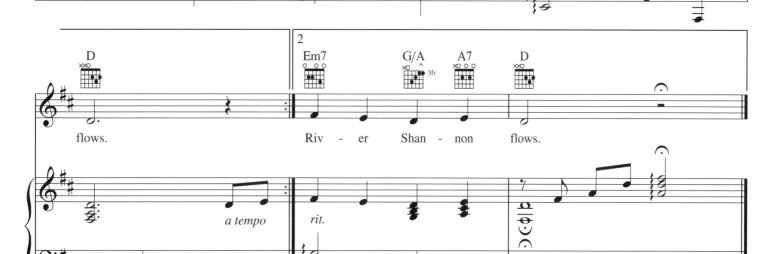

flows.   Riv - er Shan - non flows.

a tempo   rit.

THAT TUMBLE-DOWN
SHACK IN ATHLONE

Words by RICHARD W. PASCOE
Music by MONTE CARLO
and ALMA M. SANDERS

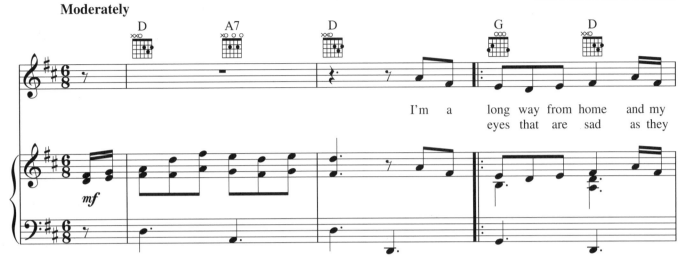

'TIS THE LAST ROSE OF SUMMER
(Air: The Groves of Blarney)

Traditional Irish Folk Melody
Words by THOMAS MOORE

TOO-RA-LOO-RA-LOO-RAL
(That's an Irish Lullaby)
from GOING MY WAY

Words and Music by
JAMES R. SHANNON

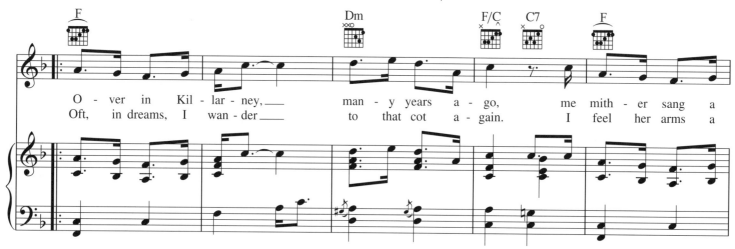

O - ver in Kil - lar - ney,___ man - y years a - go, me mith - er sang a
Oft, in dreams, I wan - der___ to that cot a - gain. I feel her arms a

song to me in tones so sweet and low. Just a sim - ple lit - tle dit - ty, in her
hug - gin' me as when she held me then. And I hear her voice a hum - min' to me

good ould I - rish way, and I'd give the world if she could sing that song to me this
as in days of yore when she used to rock me fast a - sleep out - side the cab - in

THE WEARING OF THE GREEN

Traditional Irish Folksong

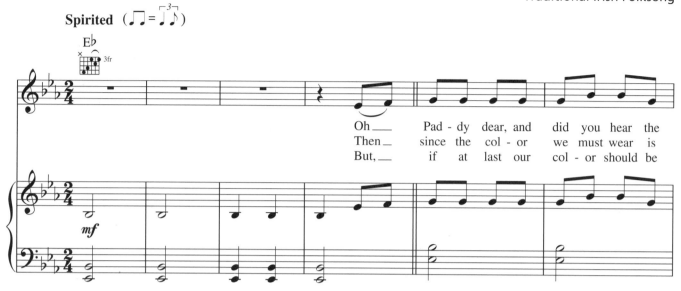

Oh ___ Pad - dy dear, and did you hear the
Then ___ since the col - or we must wear is
But, ___ if at last our col - or should be

news that's go - ing 'round? The sham - rock is for - bid by law to grow on I - rish
Eng - land's cru - el red, sure Ire - land's sons will ne'er for - get the blood that they have
torn from Ire - land's heart, her sons, with shame and sor - row, from the dear old soil will

ground. Saint ___ Pat - rick's Day no more to keep. His col - or can't be seen, for
shed. You may take the sham - rock from your hat and cast it on the sod, but
part. I've heard whis - pers of a coun - try that lies far be - yond the sea, where

WHEN HE WHO ADORES THEE

Traditional Irish Folksong

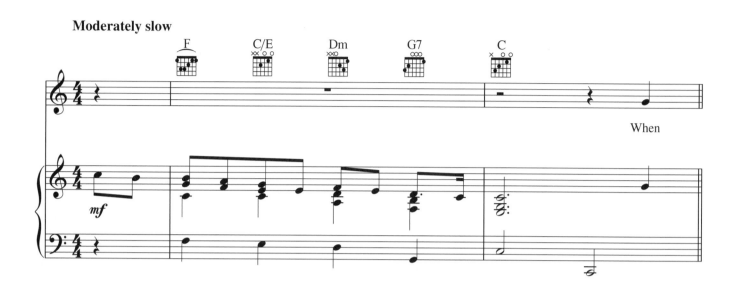

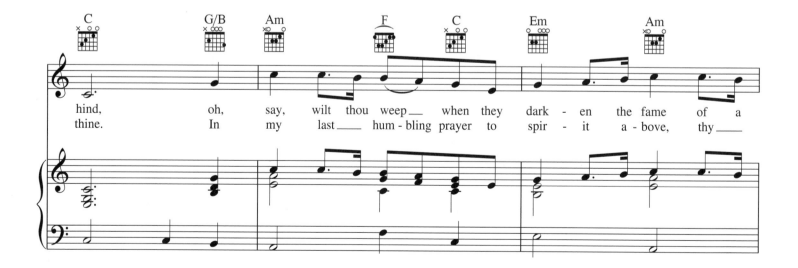

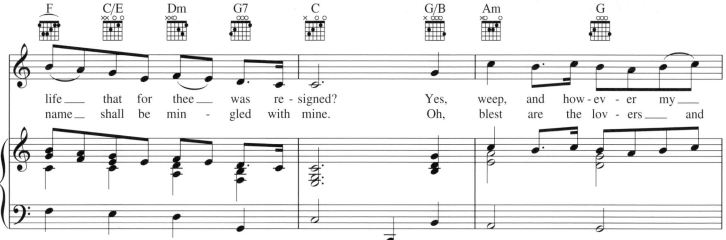

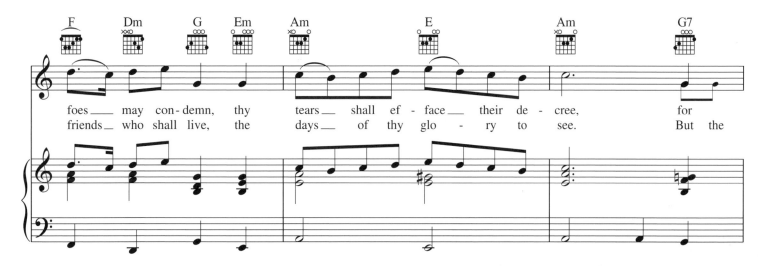

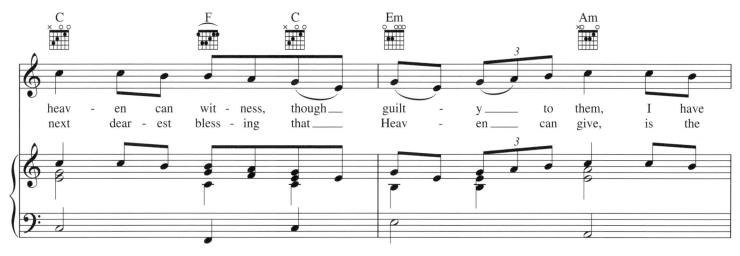

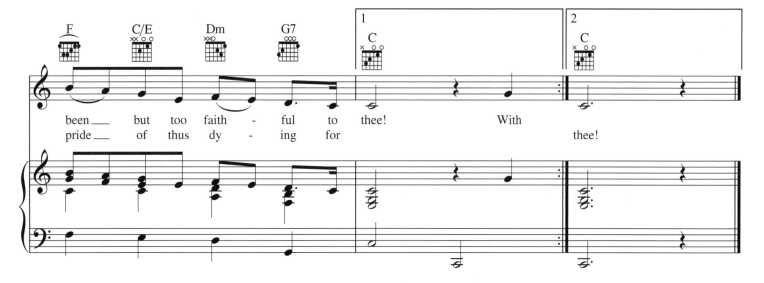

WHEN IRISH EYES ARE SMILING

Words by CHAUNCEY OLCOTT
and GEORGE GRAFF, JR.
Music by ERNEST R. BALL

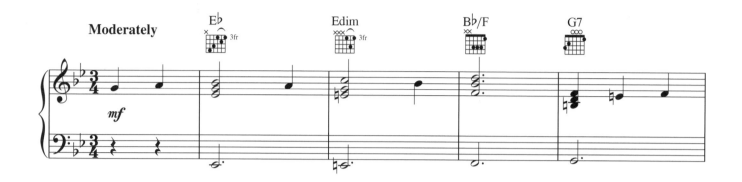

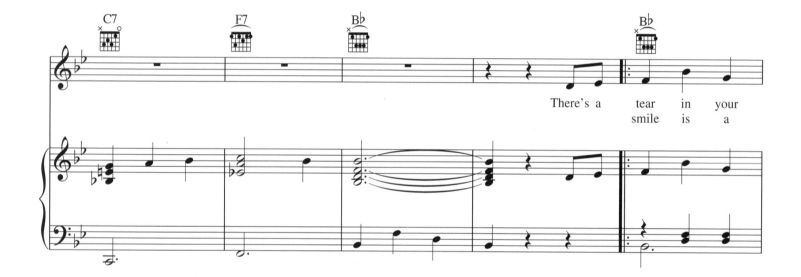

There's a tear in your
smile is a

eye, and I'm won-der-ing why, for it nev-er should be there at
part of the love in your heart, and it makes e-ven sun-shine more

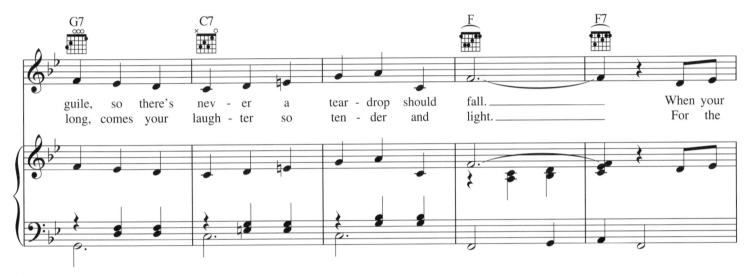

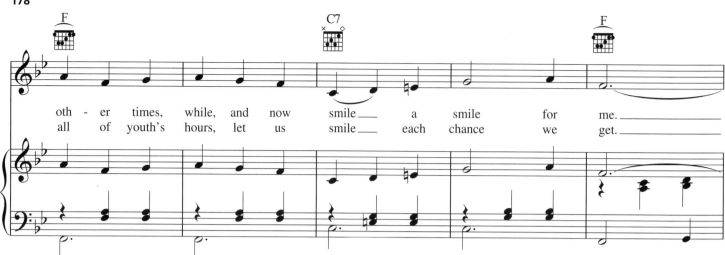

oth - er times, while, and now smile___ a smile for me.___
all of youth's hours, let us smile___ each chance for we get.___

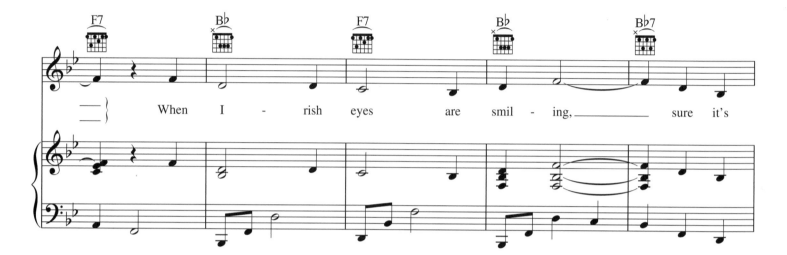

When I - rish eyes are smil - ing,_____ sure it's

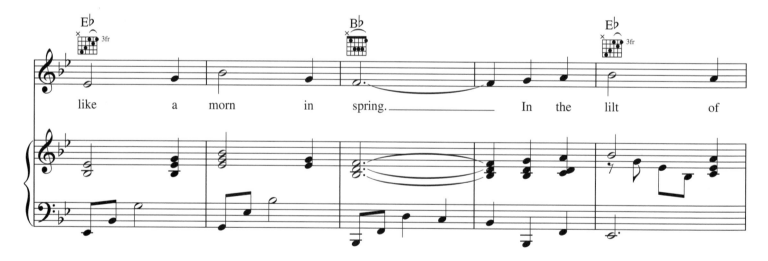

like a morn in spring._____ In the lilt of

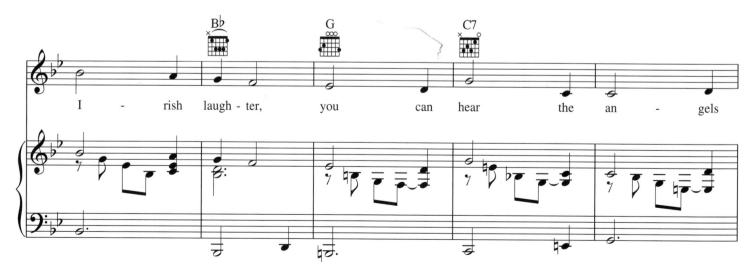

I - rish laugh - ter, you can hear the an - gels

sing. _____ When I - rish hearts are hap - py, _____

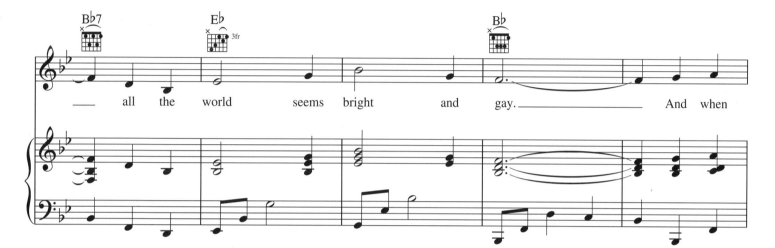

_____ all the world seems bright and gay. _____ And when

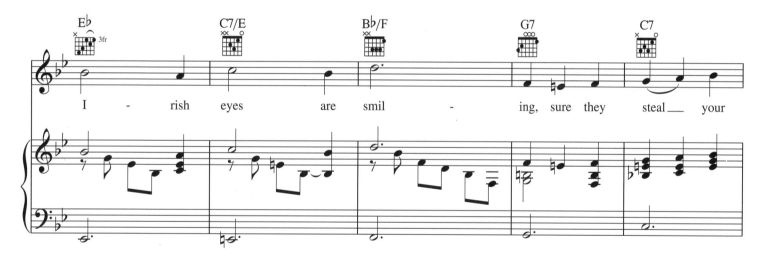

I - rish eyes are smil - ing, sure they steal __ your

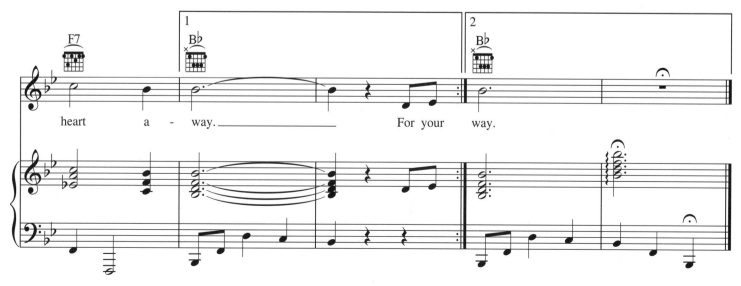

heart a - way. _____ For your way.

WHISKEY IN THE JAR

Traditional Irish Folksong

I first pro - duced me pis - tol, then pro - duced me
And she sighed and she swore,_____ she nev - er would de -
Well, I drew up - on me pis - tol, she stole a - way me

ra - pier. Sing, "Stand and de - liv - er. I am the bold - est
ceive me. The de - vil take the wom - en for they nev - er can be
ra - pier. Could - n't shoot the wa - ter, so a pris - 'ner I was

sav - er." Mush - a ring dum - ma doo - ra - ma da.
eas - y. With sha - reem dum - ma doo - ra - ma da.
tak - en. Mush - a ring dum - ma doo - ra - ma da.

Whack for the

dad - dy - o,___ whack for the dad - dy - o.___ There's whis - key in the jar.___

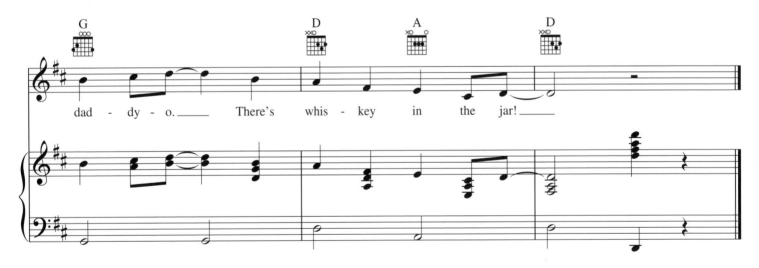

Additional Lyrics

4. Some take delight in the fishin' and the fowlin'.
Others take delight in the carriage gently rollin'.
Ah, but I take delight in the juice of the barley;
Courtin' pretty women in the mountains of Killarney.
Musha ring dumma doo-rama da.

WHO THREW THE OVERALLS IN MRS. MURPHY'S CHOWDER

Words and Music by
GEORGE L. GIEFER

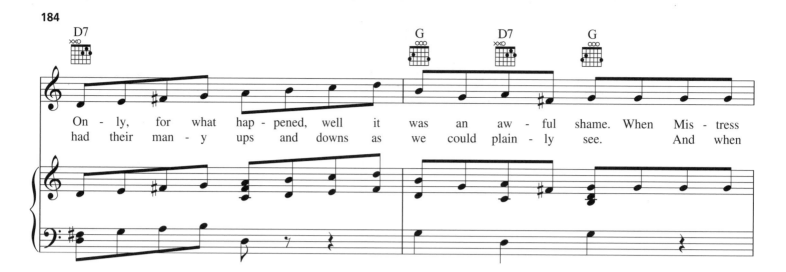

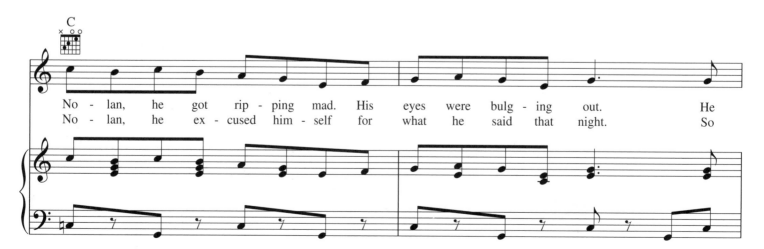

jumped up on the pi-an-o and loud-ly he did shout:
we put mu-sic to the words and sang with all our might:
"Who threw the o-ver-alls in

Mis-tress Mur-phy's chow-der?" No-bod-y spoke so he shout-ed all the loud-er: "It's an

I-rish trick, that's true. I can lick the man who threw the o-ver-alls in Mis-tress Mur-phy's

chow - der!"

They chow - der!"

YOU CAN TELL THAT I'M IRISH

from THE COHAN REVUE 1916

Words and Music by
GEORGE M. COHAN

Moderately

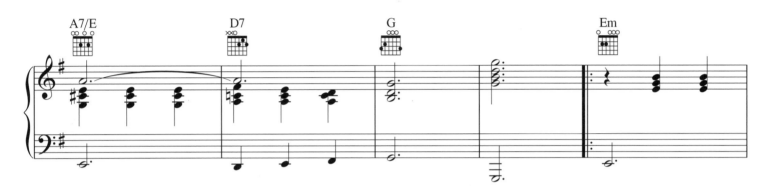

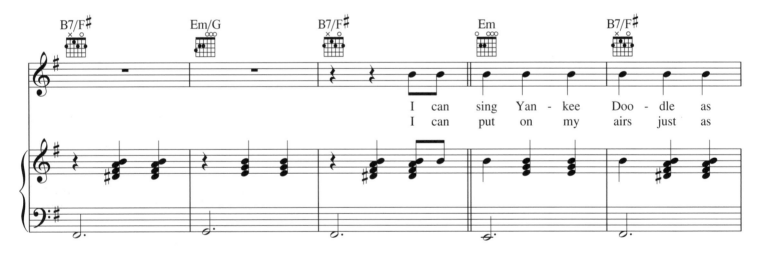

I can sing Yan - kee Doo - dle as
I can put on my airs just as

much as I please, but ev - 'ry - one seems to be wise.
much as I please, me beau - ti - ful jew - els and clothes,

As to who I am, what I am, ev - 'ry - one sees, so
but I'm I - rish, I'm I - rish, yes, ev - 'ry - one sees the

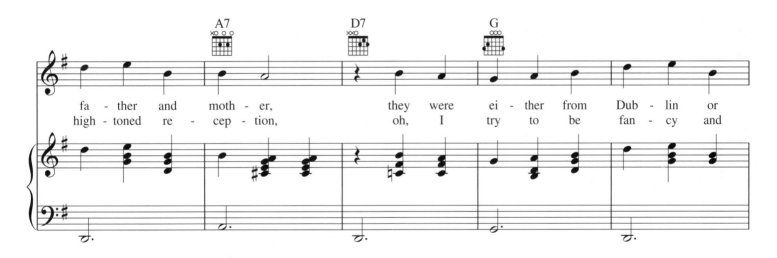

per - fect - ly plain in me eyes. You can tell that me
cute lit - tle turn of me nose. When I go to a

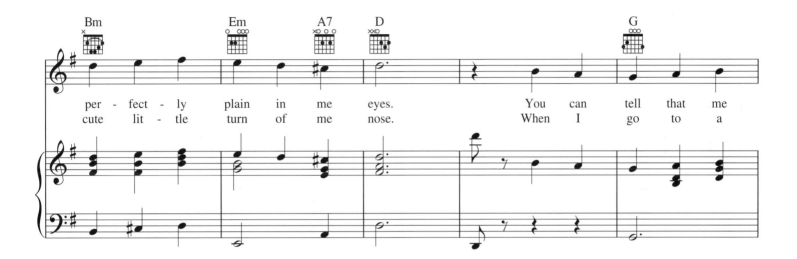

fa - ther and moth - er, they were ei - ther from Dub - lin or
high - toned re - cep - tion, oh, I try to be fan - cy and

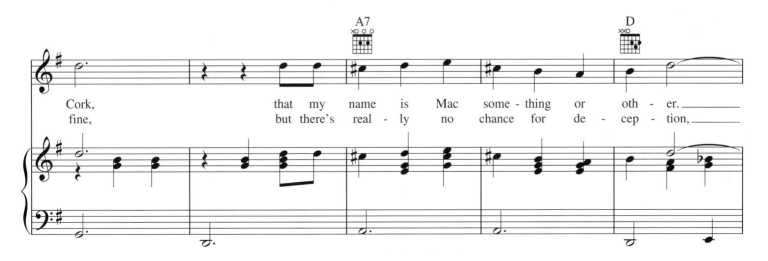

Cork, that my name is Mac some - thing or oth - er. ____
fine, but there's real - ly no chance for de - cep - tion, ____

There are hun-dreds like me in New York.
for they know I'm a real Mag - gie Cline.
You can

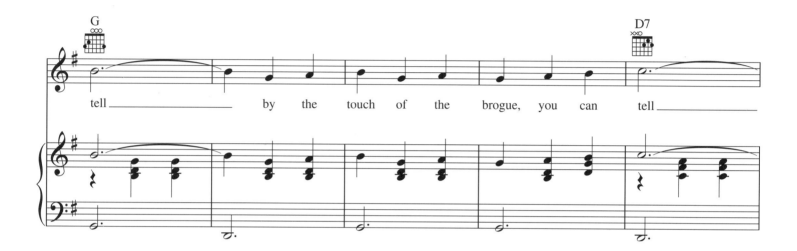

tell _____ by the touch of the brogue, you can tell _____

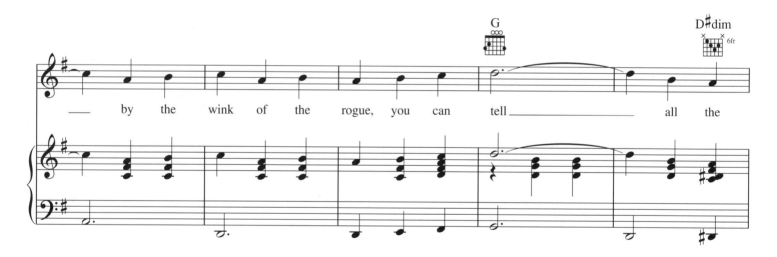

_____ by the wink of the rogue, you can tell _____ all the

while _____ by the style, _____ by the smile. _____

You can tell _____ by the wit of the talk, you can

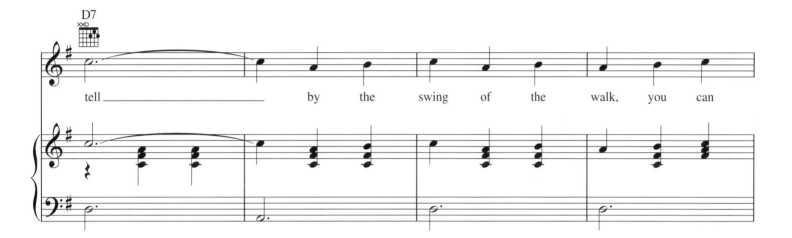

tell _____ by the swing of the walk, you can

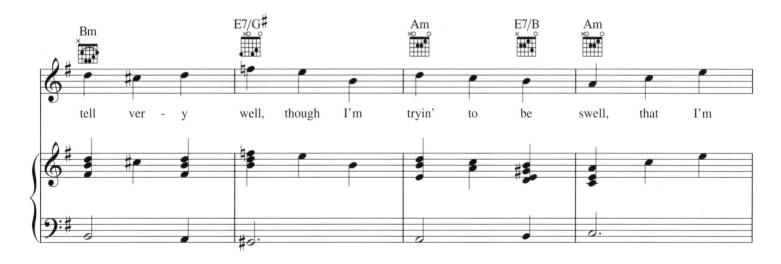

tell ver - y well, though I'm tryin' to be swell, that I'm

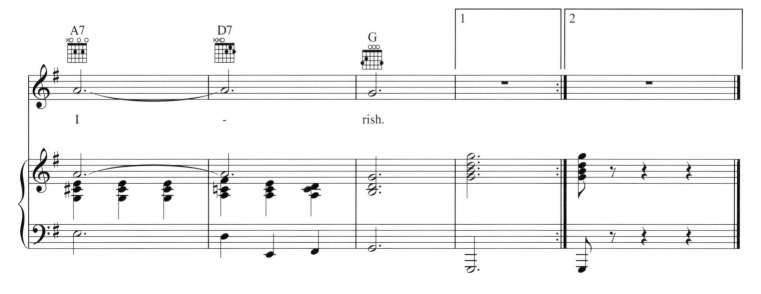

I - rish.

THE WILD ROVER

Traditional Irish Folksong

Moderately, with a lilt

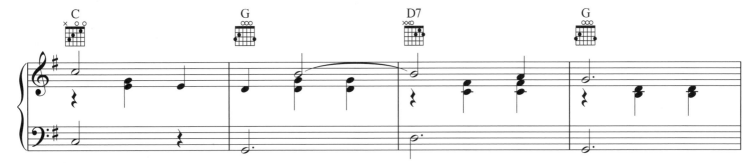

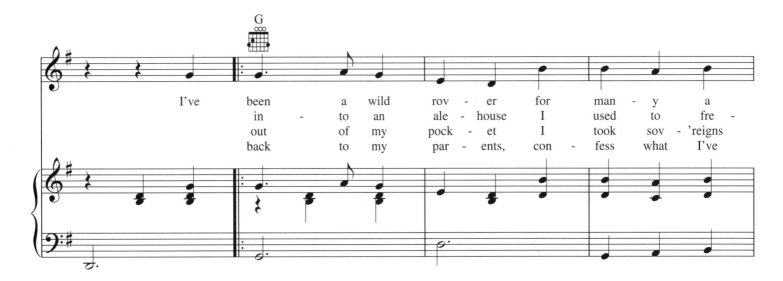

I've been a wild rov - er for man - y a
in - to an ale - house I used to fre -
out of my pock - et I took sov - 'reigns
back to my par - ents, con - fess what I've

year,_____ and I've spent all my mon - ey on
quent,_____ and I told the land - la - dy my
bright,_____ and the land - la - dy's eyes o - pened
done,_____ and____ ask them to par - don their

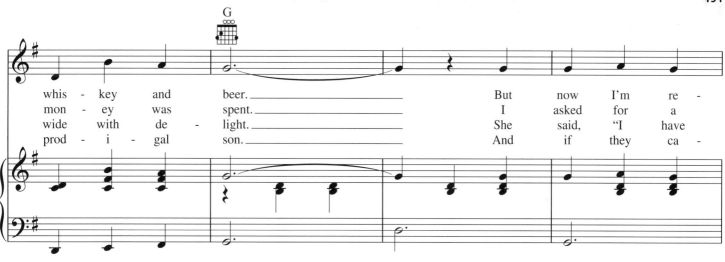

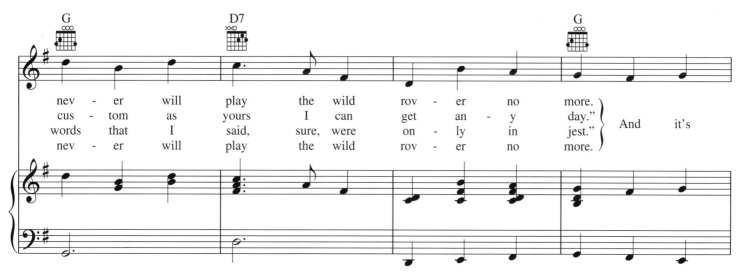

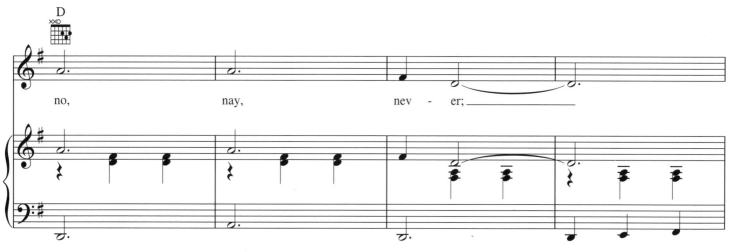

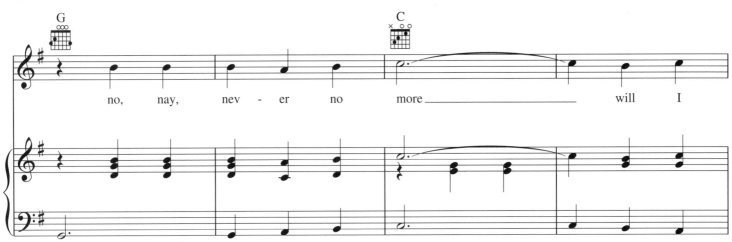

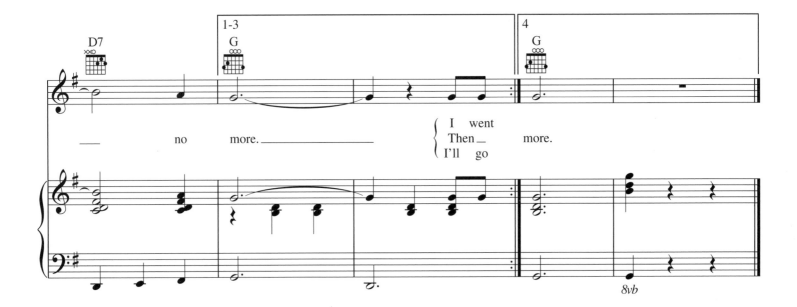